WHILE PSYCHIATRY SLEPT
REAWAKENING THE IMAGINATION IN THERAPY

WHILE PSYCHIATRY SLEPT
REAWAKENING THE IMAGINATION IN THERAPY

STORIES BASED ON REAL-LIFE CASES
by
DR. GEORGE MECOUCH, D.O.

BELLY
SONG
press

Santa Fe, New Mexico

Published by: Belly Song Press
518 Old Santa Fe Trail, Suite 1 #626, Santa Fe, NM 87505
www.bellysongpress.com

Managing editor: Lisa Blair
Editor: Jeff Braucher
Cover, interior design and production: David Moratto

While Psychiatry Slept is a book of fictional stories based on real-life cases and experiences from the author's therapy practice. Compilations of patient case histories have been used to protect privacy, and names and locales have also been altered. Permission from some patients was obtained to use their specific stories.

Mecouch, George, author.
    While psychiatry slept : reawakening the imagination in therapy : stories based on real-life cases / by Dr. George Mecouch.
    Santa Fe, New Mexico : Belly Song Press, [2018] | Includes bibliographical references.
    ISBN: 978-0-9966603-6-5 (paperback) | 978-0-9966603-7-2 (PDF) | 978-0-9966603-8-9 (Kindle/Mobipocket) | 978-0-9966603-9-6 (ePub) | LCCN: 2017949909
    LCSH: Jungian psychology. | Active imagination. | Imagination--Psychological aspects. | Dreams--Psychological aspects. | Dream interpretation--Psychological aspects--Cases. | Mind and body--Psychological aspects--Cases. | Psychotherapy--Case studies. | Psychiatry-- Methodology --Cases. | Psychotherapy--Methodology--Cases. | Psychoanalysis--Methodology --Cases. | BISAC: PSYCHOLOGY / Movements / Jungian. | PSYCHOLOGY / Movements / Psychoanalysis. | PSYCHOLOGY / Psychotherapy / General. | MEDICAL / Psychiatry / General.

LCC: BF173.J85 M43 2018 | DDC: 150.19/54--dc23

1 3 5 7 9 10 8 6 4 2

This book is dedicated to my family:
George Sr., Claire, Ken, Susan, Josh, and Megan

Without the love of family, life can be unbearable.

CONTENTS

ACKNOWLEDGMENTS

ANY WRITINGS ARE a labor of creativity, solitude, and perseverance, but also a test of relationships, as many are asked to participate and give their time freely in feedback and criticism. I have asked for this from my friends, and all have been willing and generous. I thank especially Amy Mindell, Jim Patterson, Grady Gray, Scott Sandage, Michealle Gregory, Portia Riley, Ginni Brown, Justine Taylor, Nicole Spotswood, and Rebecca Shala for their readings and useful comments.

This book is about opening up to soul and its possibilities for a different way of viewing therapy and the world. Much of this I owe to the incredible writings of C. G. Jung, James Hillman, Irvin Yalom, Mary Watkins, Arnold Mindell, and Russell Lockhart. Without their dedicated work and inspiring ideas, I would have had no shoulders to stand on.

Reading, however, is never enough, and more than anything, I owe an enduring debt to the two great mentors in my professional and personal life, Arnold ("Arny") Mindell and Russell Lockhart. Arny saw always the growing part of my personality and nurtured it through years of analysis, opening me up to the psyche in body and world. His teaching and love have been immeasurable.

Dr. Lockhart came along at a time in my life when I was floundering, yearning to write about ideas that I had long held regarding psychotherapy's current direction, but sadly believing I had no skill to tell the stories. Russ, through his unlimited patience, showed me ways to break through this block and brought out the writer within me. I cannot thank him enough.

What acknowledgment could be complete without noting the luck I have had in a wonderful family? My two children, Josh and Megan, are the loves of my life, and they have grown into exceptional adults. My life partner and wife, Susan, is the backbone of our family and has somehow put up with my moods, harebrained ideas, and the "please listen to just one last paragraph and tell me what you think" pleadings for thirty-one years. I don't know how she has done that, or what I would have done without her.

I also want to say thank you to Belly Song Press and the owners, Lisa Blair and David Bedrick: two gifted therapists who had a vision to open a small and immensely creative publishing company. They had never published a work of fictional stories, and I thank them for taking a chance on me. I would also note their tireless work and constantly cheerful disposition. They made the experience of publishing almost more enjoyable than the writing.

Additionally, I would like to say thank you to the editing skills of Jeff Braucher, whose immense knowledge and talent in the editorial arts I found humbling as I okayed his many suggestions and changes. Likewise, the visionary gifts of cover designer David Moratto need to be mentioned, as his symbolic front cover beautifully hinted as to what was to be found within the book.

Lastly, I must thank my patients. In the end they are the true mentors, refining and teaching all of us called to the profession, the art of therapy.

FOREWORD

*W*HILE *PSYCHIATRY SLEPT*, by psychiatrist George Mecouch, is a provocative title and a most intriguing volume. While the author focuses on what psychiatry fell asleep *to*—the centrality of dreams, the importance of story, the necessity of imagination, and the quest for soul—it is useful to imagine this as the dream book of a sleeping field. Some psychiatrists might experience these dreams as awakening a subtle call for things long forgotten, those yearnings for relating and working that were taken over by the seductions and promises of chemical solutions. Others might open this volume and close it abruptly, as if defending against something untoward and dangerous to one's foundation. These stories indeed might be nightmares to some who are practicing what has become an adjunctive field to the monetary dictates of the insurance industry. Others might shout out, "Irrelevant! Irrelevant!" Yet, I'm sure they are kin to the author's intentions here, not so much to reject and abandon psychiatry's genuine advances, but to remind us of and restore what psychiatry has lost, and what itself has abandoned and rejected. It is not too late; there is still time for the field to wake up, and to seek out and embrace the essence and the fruitfulness of what has gone missing.

To do this, one must go slowly and listen. Psychiatry, like most everything else, has been bewitched by *accelerationism*, as if speed itself were the road to cure. But the *art* of healing requires time, taking time, slowing down. It requires, as Keats said, not grasping after fact and reason, but staying in the midst of unknowing, uncertainty, doubts, and mystery. It is *this* ground out of which story emerges; it is *this* ground that activates the deep imagination; it is *this* ground that excites the deeper dream; it is *this* ground that serves as pathway to soul.

It may be too much to expect older practitioners to open themselves to change. Like the old church fathers, they will not look through the Galilean telescope that story-mind makes possible. Most everything animates against it. But for the newer and younger practitioners, those not yet straightjacketed in the certainties of dogma, those still open to risk, these stories of the *art* of healing may catch hold of the mind and heart, and open up possibilities for creating new and unexpected modes of working in the future.

Central to the author's argument is regaining respect and value for the dreaming mind, no matter what the pathology might be or its dimension. All practitioners should listen to the words of music legend David Bowie: "I suspect that dreams are an integral part of existence, with far more use for us than we've made of them, really. I'm quite Jungian about that. The dream state is a strong, active, potent force in our lives...the fine line between the dream state and reality is at times, for me, quite grey. Combining the two, the place where the two worlds come together, has been important in some of the things I've written, yes" (Roberts, 1999).

Artists know this fine gray line, but the value of it and the purpose for it has, it seems, been lost not only to psychiatry but to most all psychological practices. It must be recovered first by the practitioner. Only in this way will the field begin to value story again. This is the charm and extraordinary value of *While Psychiatry Slept*. Dr. Mecouch lets us in on his inside world, telling us, as Wallace Stevens would say, "not about the thing, but the thing itself."

To all practitioners of healing psychological ills of whatever nature, I encourage you to take time out, cozy up to a fire, and take these stories in. Do not be like Alice's sister who would not "pretend." Be like Alice, and take the path of the looking-glass, and see what begins to animate in your own psyche. If you let the seeds of story grow in you, you will know how to recruit the healing quality of story in those who seek healing from you.

Russell A. Lockhart, Ph.D.
Everett, Washington
May 14, 2017

INTRODUCTION

B OOMER, MY OLD and dying dog, was there in the dream, but as only dreams can do he was instead a grizzly bear. My father was there too, and we were letting Boomer out the back door as he and I had done so many times with our family dog when I was a boy growing up. Boomer seemed restless. Opening the door, I heard a deep, longing growl, and there at the bottom of the steps was a beautiful female grizzly bear. It was as if she had been waiting for Boomer. They joined each other at the bottom of the steps, growling and joyous. Suddenly, a huge blanket of white wolves appeared and put the bears on their backs, sweeping them away toward the far horizon.

From the spot on the horizon where they disappeared, a kangaroo appeared from the "land down under" and came hopping toward me, leaping into my arms. The whole while I was amazed and dumbfounded, not quite believing the unimaginable sight I was witnessing. I kept saying to my father, "Are you seeing this?" He responded throughout that he was seeing nothing unusual, just Boomer going outside to the backyard.

Dreams tend to embed a multitude of possible meanings. My sadness in losing my cherished dog, and aspects of my personal relationship with my father and our inability to connect, are all there for reflection. But this particular dream pulled me deeply toward the world and my 35-year career as a psychiatrist. I find it quite tragic that the metaphorical message in this dream is today usually missed because the current world of "fathers" and the constructed theories of the time allow very few to see the rich and incredible images from the "land down under."

Psychiatry is an amazing field. During my time in this medical specialty, I have experienced the revolution in brain science and chemistry. I have seen new medicines come forward that keep patients out of long-term hospitalizations, and research that has improved the care in schizophrenia, bipolar disorder, depression, and attention deficit disorder. Hospitals have changed from the Cuckoo's Nest-type facilities where I started my training, with bars on the windows and urine running down hallways, to current modern wards that help maintain the humanity and dignity of patients. I have seen cognitive behavioral therapy come to the forefront of training in all mental health disciplines, with the ability to put methodology in manuals for patients and therapists and make tremendous inroads in the treatment of anxiety. Dialectical behavioral therapy has now revolutionized the care of patients with para-suicidal and borderline conditions, while object relations theories have enhanced the understanding of the most virulent character pathologies.

However, in my opinion all this progress has had a dark side or at least a parallel development heading in the wrong direction. As the Age of the Brain revolution has captivated psychiatry and its training in residencies, a corresponding "loss of soul" can be increasingly witnessed. Young doctors emerge from training steeped in the latest biochemistry and DSM diagnosis but without exposure to dreams, the history of psychiatry and psychology, great literature, the body and its connection to the psyche, or any idea of alternative ways for viewing symptoms except through the prism of causality.

The idea of soul is not popular in medical circles. It is too nebulous and irrational, especially for a discipline striving to prove its reality in material and positivistic terms. But the brain is not the mind, or as I quote Jung later in these chapters, "Psychiatry has...[put] the organ, the instrument, above the function.... Function has become the appendage of its organ, the psyche the appendage of the brain.... *Modern psychiatry behaves like someone who thinks he can decipher the meaning and purpose of a building by a mineralogical analysis of its stones*" (Jung, 1969, p. 160, italics added).

It was here that Jung turned from *esse in intellectu*, the imagination that therapy was about only being in understanding or mind. However, in doing this, he did not make a 180-degree pivot into just scientism or *esse in re*, being in fact or reality. Instead his work became about *esse in anima*, being in soul. This is the middle ground of poets, fiction writers, and artists. It is the in-between or *metaxy* as the Greeks called it: a middle way that mediates between the mind and body by its language of simile and metaphor, dreams and fantasies, imagination and the as-if. It is from here that all creativity begins.

The essence of this book is about this realm. Its title, *While Psychiatry Slept*, is meant to draw attention to the fact that while psychiatry attempts to make its science about body, reality, and facts, it has fallen asleep to the realm of soul. Psychiatric and psychological training has turned against fantasy and dreams, and except for occasional writings of analysts, dreams are rarely included in psychiatric case reports. In fact, in today's theoretical underpinnings, dreams are not even considered the "royal road to the unconscious" but instead have been replaced by a dogmatic overreliance on transference and countertransference.

The stories included in this book take a much different direction. They attempt to show that psychiatry, in its amnestic slumber, has forgotten that all therapy of any depth is about dreams and "the dreaming." I would also claim that dreaming is happening all the time, not just in the dreams of the night. They arise in body symptoms, slips of the tongue, and incongruent communication signals, along with our nightly dreams, the extremities of hallucinations and delusions, synchronicities, and yes, transference and countertransference. All these conduits of the soul are filled with fanciful figures waiting to be heard and appreciated in their attempts to lead us toward the future.

The stories in this book are fictional in nature though based on cases from my practice throughout my career. This choice of fiction is purposeful, as I believe this is the primary language that the psyche prefers. The mind *stories*, or as Jung would say, it is constantly in the process of mythopoesis, the making of myth or story.

I discovered this lesson early in my career when I was having trouble learning neurology in medical school, bogged down with its dry and abstract writings. At that time I was doing a medicine rotation in a Flint, Michigan, hospital, being precepted by Dr. Jack Stanzler, a gifted teacher in the art of medicine. He gave me a book by Harry Lee Parker, M.D., titled *Clinical Studies in Neurology*. It was filled with image, beautiful prose, and sensuous description. I couldn't put it down. I became hooked on learning in this poetic medical genre, reading the works of Bernard Lown, William Carlos Williams, Lewis Thomas, Richard Selzer, Allen Wheelis, and Irvin Yalom.

The leitmotif threading its way throughout this book is that the therapies of psychiatry and psychology should be imagined as more fiction than fact, more story than science. The first chapter is "Salome and the Storytelling Mind," an attempt to imagine further into James Hillman's "The Fiction of Case History." This was a wonderful paper he wrote reflecting on whether Freud's writings might be better considered a new genre of writing called "case fiction." "Freud, in fact, had enormous literary talent and when it seemed clear that he would never win the Nobel Prize for medicine, Thomas Mann, along with other literary greats, actually encouraged the nomination of Freud for the Nobel Prize in literature. In the end he was awarded the prestigious Goethe prize" (Stone, 1995, p. 1). In this chapter I am led by Jung's muse, Salome, to revisit previous cases of mine in this light, opening up to therapy as containing character, plot, story arcs, along with protagonists, antagonists, and the mystery of the denouement.

Two chapters later, in "Jung's Lament," I again take up this idea of therapy as fiction and art, exploring two premises: first, that depth psychology is more an art than a science, and second, that expanding imagination is the primary method of therapy. This is presented by envisioning an "active imagination" between myself and C. G. Jung. In this discussion he talks of his lament from the dead, focusing on the unanswered statements from his soul that what he had been doing in his lifework was art. I am proposing, through the chapter's fictional style, that in this age of evidence-based medicine, we, as therapists, have much more to learn from writers and their fictional stories than from the abstract fantasies of science. We have made an error in our field by turning so completely to developmental theories and object-relation theorists for our method. Jung hinted as early as 1916, in his paper "The Transcendent Function," that there was a way of engaging the soul directly and allowing its voice and character to emerge.

"Jung's Lament" discusses aspects of this method from his *Red Book*, showing how he communicated with the psyche and the beginnings of his still unaccepted technique in psychiatry of a waking imaginal conversation with dreams and visions. The story also begins the exploration of the idea that dreams can be found in different "channels": not only the more typical visual and auditory channels Jung used in *The Red Book*, but also the less acknowledged channel of the body expressing itself in proprioception and movement.

The prior chapter is a story on the placebo effect titled "Frozen Healers," which centers on a debate about the placebo in medicine. This has been an area that the main field of medicine and psychiatry has ignored by not heeding Lewis Thomas, who was so impressed with the mind's healing effect on warts that he uttered this statement in *The Medusa and the Snail*: "[B]est of all, we would be finding out about a kind of super intelligence that exists in each of us, infinitely smarter and possessed of technical know-how far beyond our present understanding. It would be worth ...a National Institute of Warts," implying an institute dedicated to studying the placebo response and the healing effects of the mind (Thomas, 1995, p. 81). As psychiatry and medicine move more to concurrent documentation with doctors sitting behind computers and electronic health records, as angst about touch leads us into our fears of the "slippery slope," as medications are imagined to work completely predicated on evidence-based studies and biochemical receptors, the healing aspects of the mind will be downplayed, and its crucial place in the art of medical practice untaught.

I remember some years back going to a worldwide conference on child and adolescent psychiatry and listening to a well-known researcher talk about her studies for the use of Seroquel in the treatment of children with bipolar disorder. I will never forget when she said her statistics showed that 75% of the kids were responding significantly to Seroquel, but they couldn't get the medication FDA-approved for treatment because 73% of the children were responding to placebo. "We've got to figure out how to get the placebo response to go down so we can get this important drug approved," she said. I wondered at the time if the real research should have been why the kids responded so amazingly to placebo. What a loss!

This book now shifts to a series of stories introducing the fictional psychiatrist Thomas Harper as he treats patients with various issues ranging from anxiety and compulsions to spiritual hauntings all the way to psychosis and shamanic callings. Much of this writing pays homage to two of the distinguished psychiatric storytellers from the field, the late Allen Wheelis and the still currently writing Irvin Yalom. Both of these men mastered a genre of fictional case histories by embedding their psychological wisdom and methods in their writing. In this style, simile and metaphor, image, and sensual character are sought, and the cold abstractions of the scientistic eschewed. The great Graham Greene thought that this allows for literal memories to come out, not as journalism and purported fact, but, by being thrown into the compost heap of time, altered into the deeper truth of imagination (Olen Butler, 2006, p. 23).

The first chapter in this grouping is "Therapy and the Act of Characterization." Here I look at the importance for therapy to characterize the multiple figures that fill the soul and bring them more to the forefront, as if you were a student in a Stanislavski method-acting class. Much of my imaginations for this piece were influenced by Mary

Watkins's incredible book, *Invisible Guests*. She believes, as do I, that this moves therapy toward a less egocentric goal and opens to allowing the characters to be discovered and have a voice of their own. As Hillman says, "[L]ess about what they mean and more about what they want" (Hillman, 1983, p. 93).

"The Ashley Maker Story" was written when I awoke from a dream of a woman, Ashley Maker, who was about to come "on line," symbolically indicating that she wanted to enter my waking life. One way to work with dreams is to "dream the dream onwards" by imagining a fictional tale that might tell the story. In this instance, what if a patient came to therapy, and suddenly her dreams and the analyst's began to intertwine? What if the material coming up from the unconscious of the patient corresponded to the material that was breaking through in the therapist's life at that same moment? Whose process was it really? This story explores that possibility, showing different ways to work with dreams and countertransference, while also considering that in some cases both the patient's and the analyst's individuation are being addressed.

"Animal Eyes" is the heart of the book. I have felt since the beginning of my training that if there is any one area where the theories of psychiatry have fallen short, it has been in the area of psychoses and schizophrenia. I continue to believe, as I go on to say in the chapter, that if Jung were alive today he would still be far ahead of this current time in his views on these diagnoses. The story includes many cases of clients I have treated over the years, changed to maintain anonymity, but clearly showing that when taking the hallucinations and delusions purposefully, as if waking dreams, at times amazing therapeutic breakthroughs can occur.

In this story I talk more about what Jung referred to as the synthetic, constructive, or finalistic approach to working with patients. This under-explored method is another example of psychiatry's somnambulism, as all teaching on case formulation is based on the *causa efficiens* of Aristotle and nothing about his equally important *causa finalis*. The fictional case of Alignak and his calling to a positive integration of his so-called symptoms is an attempt to show this theory in practice and also recall this ancient, cross-cultural way extreme states of consciousness were imagined and creatively dealt with in the past.

I leave the strictly storytelling realm for a couple of chapters, doubling down on the work in "Animal Eyes" by including a paper I wrote for a conference in 1994 on working therapeutically with psychosis, and also a recent paper I submitted to a writing contest about treating psychotic states. Both of these chapters show crucial background attitudes and beliefs when working in this realm.

"The Bearded Man" is an attempt to revive interest in the body psyche, originally imagined by the Greek god of medicine, Asclepius, as it presents itself in dreams from the body, and about the body. Jung hinted at this work toward the end of his life with his statements about the psychoid unconscious and his views that "[w]e have every reason to suppose that there is only one world, where matter and psyche are the same thing" (Jung, 1975, p. 342). To imagine that the body and its organs could be dreaming and sending messages is a radical concept and would compensate nicely the current belief systems in psychosomatic medicine. Most prominent in this shift of imagination has been Arnold Mindell's work and ideas about the "dreambody" and the "dreaming" written about in his 19 books.

The story also touches on parapsychological phenomena that stretch our rational reality. Jung bookended his scientific career with experiences of the parapsychological: first, the writing of his doctoral dissertation, "On the Psychology and Pathology of So-Called Occult Phenomena," and then having an experience close to the end of his life in which he encountered his doctor, floating up as an image from the direction of Europe, framed by a golden laurel wreath, and as he stood before Jung, he assumed "his primal form, as a basileus of Kos," and delivered a protest that Jung had no right to leave the earth and must return (Jung, 1973a, p. 292). Between these two events, Jung had multiple other experiences that were unexplainable in consensus terms.

It also shows the use of etymology as a surprising method in working with dreams, and helps us to realize that though our Newtonian causal theories remain quite useful, they do not begin to encompass all the amazing stories that can walk in the door of our everyday practices.

I close with a lyrical and fun chapter on synchronicity titled "Castle Callings." Another way the dreaming world can present itself is by coming through a world channel in a surprising, apparently acausal way. This is seen in the first case in the book when Julia and I experience the blue jay hitting the window, corresponding to her thoughts at that moment. In "Castle Callings" it is imagined as a series of events that are too meaningful to be cast off in the "nothing but" rational explanation of coincidence.

It seems only appropriate to our topic that the introduction should end as it began, with a dream. I was struggling with writer's block for months while trying to complete the "Jung's Lament" portion of the book. One morning I awoke with this dream: *Dr. Jung was with me while in his later years, moving slowly yet clearly still quite vibrant. Jung and I began to speak about what the problem was with my writing and what was holding me back. I talked about my work hours, but said that these had improved and were no longer an issue. I told him that I was sure it was my ongoing struggle with being disciplined, but to my surprise he did not agree. He suddenly turned and faced me and with an impish grin said, "You must write from your madness, as I did." He seemed to do a little jig and then added, "How do you think I wrote so many books?"*

What does Jung mean that he wrote from his madness and what does it mean to write from mine? Does it symbolize writing from your deepest passions and beliefs, from where you feel the anger that something is terribly wrong? Could the roots of the word *madness* give us a hint to the answer?

Mad derives from various languages: *gemaedde,* or "out of one's mind," implying outside the typical collective views, seeming to be foolish and stupid; *ga-moita* and *mutare,* meaning "to change." Mad births also from *migrare,* "to change one's residence." An interpretation of "writing from your madness" could be imagined as: "Writing from our foolish self, the one that seems stupid and not agreed upon by normal views, leads to a possible change in direction from the current consensus of ideas and theories. It opens us to the ability to change where we are sitting in our resident beliefs and see the world from different vantage points." It may take a touch of madness to do this.

So I am asking the reader to grant me this foolishness and have an open mind about my attempt at bringing dreams back to their rightful place—the centerpiece of all psychological theory. It is from here that the original meaning of *psycho-therapy* is remembered: "therapy of the soul."

SALOME AND THE STORYTELLING MIND

STRETCHED MY back and yawned, then glanced warily at the clock. It was late on a Friday evening, and I had just finished reading Hillman's seminal paper "The Fiction of Case History." His reimagining of psychotherapy and its practice as closer to literature than science was like opening up to one of Stan Grof's holotropic breathing experiences. What if therapy were more fiction than fact, more story than theory? What if the purpose of therapy was to be told into story and given a plot to live by? Not sure where to begin, I looked down and saw my dog Riley sleeping contentedly on the floor beside me. The thought of a short siesta before tackling such a paradigm-shifting idea felt just right....

The fire licked the sides of the crater, sometimes leaping almost to the rim. I flinched with its rise and hit my head on the stone wall behind me. My eyes began to acclimate to the surroundings, and I realized I was sitting on the edge of an abyss that seemed to reach to Hades. The bench was narrow and carved into a sheer cliff wall. I felt a soft touch on my arm and turned to find Salome sitting beside me. Her constant companion, the black snake, was at our feet. I had just met her a week or two before in a dream, though as she told me then, she had been trying to gain my attention for many years, dressed in different personified disguises. She seemed to know right away what brought me again so quickly to her. "I am pleased that poetry has finally found you," she said quietly. "I know you have many questions."

I sat for a moment with my eyes shut, trying to calm the rush of thoughts, but before I could ask for logical explanations, Salome spoke, saying, "Let's proceed through *memoria*. Remember, my sisters and I have always been the hidden muses throughout history for all who have asked these questions. You have read many of them and have always been drawn to their way of thinking. Plato and Blake, Rilke and Jung, Neruda, Hillman, Mindell, Lockhart, and Watkins—they have all been mentors to you. It has just been hard for you to listen." Salome touched my arm and asked me to shut my eyes. Suddenly memories of my patient's dreams and stories came rushing back.

"Can you see her sitting there?" Salome asked.

"I can," I said in surprise. It was Julia sitting across from me in a session from so many years ago. I began to tell Salome what a lovely young woman Julia was, tragically caught in the midst of recurrent psychotic episodes. She had been quite drawn to the spiritual side of existence, so much so that she had shunned relationships with men. She told me that day that she might be pregnant and smiled saying she had decided that if she was pregnant, she would keep the child and become a mother. I remember the next moment vividly. A blue jay hit the window. Over and over again, it pecked and banged. Julia's face blanched. I asked her what she knew of blue jays. She said they steal the eggs from nests and eat them. She then revealed that at the moment the blue jay had come, she had a thought that she was a disgusting sinner for considering having a baby.

As the reverie ended I heard Salome ask, "Was this experience science?"

"No, it doesn't qualify as science."

"But was it useful," Salome responded quickly. "My criterion is not verifiable science in this sense, but we must ask: Is the story or experience heuristic? Does it lead to a deeper understanding and a different way of holding her psychotic experiences?"

I could begin to see the consequences of this shift in therapy. The truth could never be proved in the same way as biology or geology, but instead was based on how the story carried the person into life. That story created an opening in Julia's therapy to come back again to what we now called "Blue Jay Man," the one who would take away her baby and the wishes for her own existence. We spent time characterizing him as if he were an antagonist in a novel, defining him with face, name, thoughts, voice, and a belief system. He took on life, yet she was now no longer identified with him. These moves allowed us to look for him and identify the when, how, and why of his coming and going. She began to find a thread of meaning in her constant suffering.

Salome smiled at my thoughts. She reached over and touched my arm again, saying, "Let's go further."

Another memory came flooding back. He sat with his back pushed rigidly against my couch, seemingly afraid of losing contact. "It's Robert," I told Salome, "a man with a very difficult childhood history." My memory continued as I asked Robert about his sitting posture, and he told me of the fear that he had a hole in his back and unless it was covered, his spirit would fly out. He told me of this feeling, which had begun in childhood, and the way he had always slept carefully on his back with the covers pulled tight to his neck. He also told of how difficult it had been to tell me because the last therapist to whom he divulged this history said he most likely had a multiple personality disorder. That therapist also implied it was obvious what the hole in his back referred to.

After assuring him that there were better ways of storying these fears than his previous therapy had presented, I asked him to try something completely different. What if he incubated a dream in the old Asclepian tradition? "I'll never forget the dream he brought in," I excitedly told Salome. "*He was in an airplane with three other men who were all him. The plane was flying over the Alps. There were jagged mountain cliffs below. Suddenly the plane turned and headed straight toward the mountains as if to crash. But then just as suddenly, it was approaching for a landing, except now it was heading into a hole or cave in the side of the mountain. The mountain was on its side and looked just like a spinal column. Once inside he and the other three Roberts got out and stood facing the four directions, with him to the north. There in front of him was his beating heart, and he knew now he was inside his own body. Just to the right of the heart was a little five-year-old boy wrapped in a gold liquid gel, alive but as if in suspended animation. Robert heard frightening noises to his right. There was a long tunnel leading into the blackness, and it was from here the noises were coming. He knew that he would have to go down this tunnel before the little boy could be freed.*"

"Can you now see the difference between story and fact?" Salome asked. "This is crucial. What you have been practicing for years with clients has not been science, it has been fiction. The mind *stories*. It is set up that way, as I helped Jonathan Gottschall to realize in his book *The Storytelling Animal*. Look at what happened when you were open to a different way of seeing and fictioning: open to not reducing his symptom to only the story of trauma and to not giving him the plot of pathology and multiple personality. Instead, by creating the opportunity for his imagination to have its own voice, you enabled a different story to come through. Remember what one of your favorite mentors has said: 'It is not a matter of indifference whether one calls something a "mania" or a "god." To serve a mania is detestable and undignified, but to serve a god is full of meaning and promise'" (Jung, 1967, p. 38).

Salome and I sat quietly on the bench for quite some time after the memories subsided. I had a sense of appreciation for all she had shown me. She smiled silently and gave me a good-bye look before touching my arm one last time.

I awoke on the floor next to Riley. I looked at the clock. Only a few minutes had passed. I touched a warm spot on my left arm and remembered Salome and the *memoria*. I had been dreaming. Or had I?

FROZEN HEALERS

"For some patients, though conscious that their
position is perilous, recover their health simply
through their contentment with the physician."
—Hippocrates (cited in Lown, 1996, p. 3)

I SPLASHED COLD water against my face with only a small hope of waking
fully for morning rounds. I was late for Dr. Hartley Lansfeld, M.D.,
and I knew there would be hell to pay. He did not tolerate the chief
resident of the Internal Medicine Department, specializing in cardiology, being tardy for his cardiac surgery team rounds, even with a patient care excuse, and I had a good one. I had been up all night in the
Cardiac Care Unit tending a patient suffering with paroxysmal atrial
tachycardia. In this condition the heart speeds up to 140–160 beats
per minute in sinus rhythm. This is not normally life threatening, but
in this case we had just performed surgery on his congenitally leaky
aortic valve. The chance of pulmonary emboli was now at risk.

What made this case odd, however, were the bizarre drops in body
temperature. Billy, the 18-year-old I sat up with last night, had been doing well post surgically until shortly after rounds yesterday morning
with Dr. Lansfeld. He and I had come to see Billy and his mother with
a phalanx of medical students, interns, and residents trailing behind.
Billy had asked the good doctor, with obvious apprehension, how he
was doing after Lansfeld had finished the examination. "You're fine.
You have some ectopic beats and a run or two of tachycardia, but nothing important," the preeminent surgeon said with his typical bedside

5

brevity and missing compassion. He then turned to his following and questioned, "So what would we expect to see if our patient goes sour? What findings on auscultation and patient presentation?"

A third-year student quickly blurted out, "An S3 gallop." Everyone laughed, and Lansfeld asked the intern to tell the lowly medical student why this was such an incompetent reply.

"First of all, it would be normal in young athletes, but that's not the case here with the patient's premorbid heart condition," the intern replied confidently. "It would then indicate postoperative congestive heart failure and a very poor prognosis. If this patient went sour post surgically, this is not what we would expect."

"And what would you expect to hear and see, young man?" Lansfeld bellowed, giving the third-year student a look that clearly indicated, "What are you doing on my service, nincompoop!"

"You would auscultate ectopic beats with PVCs seen on ECG, possibly atrial fibrillation. He would present as tachypneic and with complaints of feeling chilled."

"Adequate," retorted Lansfeld. "Adequate" was the most you could ever expect from the great man. As the white-coated horde turned to leave, Dr. Lansfeld gave Billy's mother one last morsel of his healing wisdom. "Don't look so nervous, I did a great surgery on your son."

As I headed toward the door I saw the look on Billy's face and stopped for an extra minute. "You okay, buddy?" I said, knowing the show that had just occurred in his room would leave anyone upset.

"Doc, you have been good to me this whole time. I didn't understand all that heart speak. Could I still die?" Billy nervously queried. "All that atrial something and galloping whatever didn't sound good."

I laughed and jostled his hair, saying, "Your heart sounds great and the surgery fixed everything. You're going to be galloping yourself in no time." He took a huge breath of relief, and his mother, who was standing next to him, mouthed a thank-you. Now, as I wheeled for the door to catch the "white coats" before being missed, Billy had a healing morsel of his own to share.

"Hey, Doc, you're a great doctor. Don't ever become like your mentor. He's cold, man!"

Shooting through the door and about to head into a dead sprint, suddenly I was nose to nose with Dr. Lansfeld. He and the coats had held a case discussion just outside the patient's door and overheard my interaction with Billy.

"You see, students, Dr. Bauman thinks medical practice and outcome hinges on his imitating the famous medical painting *The Doctor*. For those of you not aware of this anachronism, the physician sits by the bedside of the sick patient, doing nothing, chin in hand, a look of consternation on his face, waiting. Isn't that right, Doctor?" Lansfeld said with his most virulent sarcasm.

"Doctor Lansfeld, I don't think this is the proper place for this discussion," I said, trying to avoid a scene.

"I insist! You don't think that my surgical acumen is what saves patients' lives, and what will make your young Billy boy gallop, as you said," Lansfeld shot back with the famous "the science of technology is all" salvo, without care for time or place.

"You know I'm not a Luddite, sir, but I do believe that bedside manner, compassion, and the placebo response have a large and unappreciated effect on healing and surgical outcome," I replied, trying to maintain some semblance of calm as Lansfeld was attempting to publicly shame me.

"Ah, I knew we would get to the placebo mumbo jumbo soon enough," Lansfeld harrumphed. "You see, everyone, Dr. Bauman did a rotation with that quack Bernard Lown. He used to be a respected cardiologist, but then he wrote that abomination of a so-called scientific book, *The Lost Art of Healing*. He and our chief resident here are now the main card-carrying members of the 'cardiologist's for healing by hand holding' club." Snickers could be heard from the coats, but before I could respond, nurses were running for Billy's room, his mother at the door screaming, "Please help!"

Billy was sitting up in bed, an ashen look on his face and clearly struggling with his breathing. Quick examination recorded a heart rate of 148, blood pressure at 155/90, and temperature of 97.1. Between attempts at breaths he mumbled, "Doc, I'm so cold!"

I sat up most of the night with Billy, his arrhythmia coming and going, but slowly he reached stability and the last of his chills receded. Finally, shortly before I could go and get some sleep myself, he awoke and told me he had had the oddest dream: *A man that looked like Dr. Lansfeld was standing over him to do an examination, but somehow Billy was the one doing the examining, being able to look into the doctor's chest, seeing in place of his heart a wash cloth with two huge female hands wringing and squeezing the water out of it. There was a pile of embers just below, still glowing but almost going out.*

"What does that mean, Doc?" Billy asked, bleary-eyed, but with all his vitals now stable.

"I don't know, Billy. They don't give you much dream work in cardiology," I said, laughing. "I'll have to ask one of my psychiatric buddies. It seems like an important dream."

"I know a little about dreams," he responded. "My dad was an analyst before he died, and used to ask me my dreams at the breakfast table every morning. He said they were very important, and as I got older he tried to teach me some about how to understand them. He told me they were like poetry, speaking the language of metaphor, and you could never go wrong by sticking close to the image."

"Wow, are you going to follow in your dad's footsteps?" I asked, impressed with his interest and knowledge. "Why don't you take a shot at what you think this dream means. What do you think your dad would say?"

"The answer to your first question is that I hope to attend Michigan State next year where they have a very famous psychology department and graduate school. It all depends on how my heart is doing. My plan is to go on and get my Ph.D. after that and become a

Jungian analyst like my dad. As for the dream, I'm not sure, but I think he would call it an 'objective dream.' This means it might be about the real Dr. Lansfeld and not about the inner doctor inside me. I wonder if he has literal heart disease from the image of the squeezing washcloth, possibly angina or maybe even an impending heart attack. It also could just be metaphorical and that he is not noticing painful emotions and feelings that may be going on every day and that he is close to having his whole inner feeling life burn out for good."

"Whoa, Billy! You're good at that. Your dad taught you well," I said, amazed.

"We did it every day for as long as he lived," Billy replied, his eyes tearing up. "Mom and I miss him greatly. He was a good dad."

"I am sure he was and is quite proud of you. I know that I'm quite impressed. Listen, you're stable now and doing well, so I'm going to catch a quick power nap before morning rounds and will be back to see you with the team and transfer you out of CCU this morning."

"Okay, Dr. Bauman, see you then. And you might want to ask Dr. Lansfeld about his physical health. My dad said the most important part of dream work was not just the understanding, but what you did with it in your everyday life afterwards."

The bed in the residents' call room had never felt so welcoming. I smiled, thinking about telling Dr. Lansfeld, the ultimate science guy and rational enlightenment man, that his patient had dreamt about him and was recommending an angiogram based on his dream interpretation. I also began to muse on all I had learned about taking the soft signs of medicine more seriously while on the rotation I had done just the year before with the distinguished cardiologist Bernard Lown. Dr. Lown's teaching was like nothing else I had experienced in medical school or residency, and I was lucky that my department chair, who had gone to school with Dr. Lown, was able to arrange for me to study in Boston for three months with the great man.

I remembered the first day on his service as we went to see a Chinese gentleman who was accompanied by his lovely wife for his checkup. This was the day Dr. Lown had taught me the art of listening, what he considered the essence of the underappreciated term "bedside manner." I could still hear him saying, "Bauman, to learn the art of medicine you must learn to listen. I mean effective listening, not just with the ears but with all the senses. Practicing this art requires not just 'expert knowledge of disease, but an appreciation of the intimate details of a patient's emotional life.... To succeed in healing, a doctor must be trained, above all else, to *listen*'" (Lown, 1996, p. 9, italics added).

Mr. Goyang was a man that Dr. Lown had been seeing for years with apparently stable angina pectoris. On each yearly visit he was pronounced fit and told to return a year later. But on this visit, though he claimed to be swimming every day and without chest pain, Dr. Lown felt something did not seem quite right. His wife, who had accompanied him without fail on these visits over the past ten years, would not look at Dr. Lown or her husband and stared the whole time at the ceiling. The real listening and crucial information was in this incongruent signal. She had always been quite attentive on previous visits, and so as Dr. Lown sent Mr. Goyang out to the consulting room for the post-exam conference, he held Mrs. Goyang back to ask her about her unusual countenance. Sure enough, when pressed, she admitted fearfully, stepping outside the bounds of her husband's wishes, that he was not exercising because of increased chest pain and was popping nitroglycerine throughout the day. Dr. Lown arranged an immediate treadmill stress test, and because of its findings Mr. Goyang was shortly having a coronary angiogram and then emergency coronary bypass surgery. He recovered uneventfully (Lown, 1996, pp. 10–12).

His words and teaching continued to echo as I tried to calm myself from a difficult day and find some sleep. "You see, Dr. Bauman," I remembered Lown saying, "'in this modern epoch, the growing intimacy between medicine and science promotes an illusion that they are identical. It leads doctors to trivialize the importance of bedside manner, fosters neglect of comprehensive history-taking, and diminishes the investment of self in promoting humane interactions with patients'" (Lown, 1996, p. 122).

Lown was also a huge believer in the effect of words, both "words that maim" and "words that heal." He spoke often about "faith and optimism" in treatment and their crucial "life-giving properties." I remembered one late night in the hospital when he invited me back to his office for a beer before heading home, and we talked about the amazing power of the mind and the placebo response. That morning we had treated a patient who suffered from atrial fibrillation with a procedure called cardioversion, involving the discharge of electrical pulses across the chest to abolish any abnormal heart rhythm. We also cured, to my amazement, her chronic back pain.

I had been with him on rounds the day before when she said she didn't much care about the arrhythmia but was hoping the procedure would get rid of her back pain. She was actually quite vehement, saying, "I don't want to undergo this cockamamy what-you-call-it unless it helps my back pain. I want a straight answer. Will the electric treatment cure my back?"

Lown replied without hesitation, "Of course it will!" (Lown, 1996, pp. 108–109).

After the cure I asked him, "How could that have happened? It makes no sense physiologically."

"That's what is so stunning," Lown responded. "There is so much about the effects of the mind we do not know. I remember speaking with Lewis Thomas years ago about warts and how they could go away with hypnosis and suggestion."

I quickly jumped in saying, "I got a huge wart on my hand when I was seven and my dad put Merthiolate on it and told me it would be gone the next morning and it was!"

"Yes, that is what can be so incredible. How is this possible?" Lown wondered. "I read of a shocking experiment that would never be allowed today in the more stringent patient restrictions involving research." He reached for Anne Harrington's book *The Placebo Effect* on his shelf and said, "Here's the passage: 'Back in 1950, Stewart Wolf reported giving ipecac (an emetic) to a severely nauseous pregnant woman and vigorously assuring her that this was medication that would help her; a balloon in her stomach showed that her stomach began contracting normally within minutes after treatment'" (Harrington, 1997, p. 6).

Dr. Lown and I sat quietly for a while, sipping our beers, when he shared another incredible story of the power of the unconscious mind and its words. He remembered, from some years back, one of the most amazing cases he was ever involved in: "The patient was a sixty-six-year-old man who was critically ill. He had a heart attack about two weeks before I first saw him and still was in cardiac intensive care, having developed just about every complication possible. Nearly half of his heart muscle had been destroyed and he was now suffering with congestive heart failure. With his left-sided failure the blood was backing up into his lungs and making it impossible to breathe. He also had no appetite, was dizzy when standing, couldn't sleep because of lack of oxygen, and with lips purplish blue from insufficient oxygen in his blood, periodically gasped for air as though drowning. There was little hope and all that we tried had been of little use. A 'do not resuscitate' order was placed on his chart" (Lown, 1996, p. 81).

"One morning he felt better and I moved him to a step-down unit so that possibly it might be less stressful and he could get more sleep. Within a week he was discharged and I lost track of him. Six months later he showed up in my office, looking in remarkably good health, his heart still badly damaged but free of congestion and largely asymptomatic.

"'A miracle,' I said.

"'Hell no, this ain't no miracle,' he responded. He then told me he was aware that we had been at our wits' end in the hospital and did not know what to do for him. He thought we had given up hope and his goose was cooked. Then he said, 'On Thursday morning, April twenty-fifth, you came in with your gang and put your stethoscope on my chest and encouraged everyone to listen to my "wholesome gallop."

I figured that if my heart was still capable of a healthy gallop, I couldn't be dying and I got well'" (Lown, 1996, p. 82).

ᘉ

Water still dripping from my face, I ran a brush through my hair, took a swig of mouthwash, and managed to grab my stethoscope on the way out the door. I realized it had been the page of the hospital loud speaker that had abruptly awakened me from my reveries. Lansfeld always started morning rounds at the CCU; I would head there first.

Dr. Lansfeld was just entering the cardiac unit with his cohort of trainees when I caught up with them.

"I am glad you could find time to join us, Dr. Bauman," Lansfeld sarcastically greeted me.

I apologized for my tardiness, but quickly decided not to make any excuses, even though I had a well-deserved one, because the look on his face appeared even less welcoming than usual. It gave the impression of his being tired and worn, his eyes drooping with dark circles, his lips drawn tight and thin. Gossip among staff had it that there was serious trouble at home, possibly talk of divorce. I was also more aware today than usual of his physique. He was a tall, thin man with long arms, long legs, and even long fingers, yet despite these odd body proportions, Lansfeld cut a powerful presence, always dressed exquisitely in the most expensive of fitted suits and carrying himself with an air of superiority.

I was always aware of his having Abraham Lincoln–style features, sans his famous beard and legendary compassion. Some thought that Lincoln had suffered with a rare disorder called Marfan syndrome, and until that moment I had never associated that possibility with Dr. Lansfeld. I knew that people with Marfan could have very serious heart complications, and Billy's dream quickly entered my mind. Could his dream premonition be correct?

Suddenly I was thrown back into the present moment as Lansfeld's rapier-like verbal attack took aim in my direction.

"Dr. Bauman, if you are done sleepwalking and unconsciously staring at me, you could start to pretend you are my chief resident and tell us about our patient Billy Handle," he said. "As you remember from yesterday everyone, Dr. Bauman was confusing the patient's reasons for improvement to placebo and not to the skillful surgery I performed. Billy developed a noncomplicated, stress-related arrhythmia that Dr. Bauman fretted about so much that he stayed up holding the patient's hand all night and forgot to sleep. Does that about sum it up, Doctor?"

Before I could reply, Billy spoke up: "Dr. Bauman, did you tell Dr. Lansfeld about my dream?"

I shook my head no, whispering, "Now is not the right time, Billy."

"The right time for what!" Lansfeld exploded, red-faced. "Are you gossiping about me to patients and undermining my authority? I will have you thrown out of this residency."

Suddenly, his face turned ashen as he reached for his chest and fell to the floor of the CCU. The action was swift. Our already being in the cardiac care unit did not require a code blue call, and resuscitation efforts were in process in seconds. Dr. Lansfeld was in ventricular fibrillation and sudden cardiac death was his possible fate. The team responded well, and cardiac defibrillation saved his life. We set him up for an immediate angiogram and probable emergency surgery. His EKG was stable and he was no longer having the extra ventricular systolic beats, but the cardiac enzyme blood tests did show that he had had a heart attack. The next hour was crucial.

We got him tucked in on the cardiac unit, and ironically his bed was right next to Billy's. Even with all the excitement, Billy had now fallen back to sleep, exhausted from his surgery and having been awake for much of the night with the treatment of his arrhythmia. Sadly, when I called Dr. Lansfeld's wife she informed me that she had already filed for divorce and that their only daughter and he were estranged. No one from the family would be coming in to visit. Her last comment to me as we hung up the phone was, "He is a cold man, Dr. Bauman. I don't know how I stayed married to him this long."

I sat by his bedside, feeling the weight of his isolation and aloneness. How does a man this talented make decisions that leave him so unloved by the most important people in his life? As I sat wondering about these twists of fate, Dr. Lansfeld awoke, and staring at me intensely, suddenly reached out and grabbed my hand.

"Dr. Bauman, I know you saved my life. Thank you," he said softly, squeezing my hand. "Would you please call my family and let them know what happened and that I'm okay?" he asked.

"I did call your wife and let her know. She said they wouldn't be able to come at this time." He silently turned his face away from mine, a tear visible on his cheek. He now noticed Billy sleeping in the next bed.

"I don't believe in dreams, but while I was asleep, *I dreamt I had an S3 gallop and that Billy was holding my hand and telling me love and compassion would be my cure.* I find it theoretically amazing that after I have so categorically disparaged you and Lown and the famous *Doctor* painting, that my dream would be so blatantly transparent in its message." His usual hard expression had softened, and he looked apologetic. I detected a profound change in him. "I am no fool and know I'm going to need surgery, possibly later today. If you can call my partner, Dr. Wilfred—he's the most gifted of cardiac surgeons—but I would ask that you assist him. I'm starting to think that surgery without the healing compassion of the physician is only half the cure."

The surgery went marvelously well, and the damage to his heart was minimal. There was no evidence of any of the heart consequences of Marfan, and angioplasty and a stent were all that was necessary. What was most exciting was the change in Dr. Lansfeld. Remarkably, he was the nurses' favorite in the CCU, and every day Billy would come in to play chess with him; they had become the best of friends. He had connections at Michigan State and was able to get Billy an interview at the school. In between chess moves they could be overheard talking about their dreams from the night before, with Billy now playing the teacher to Lansfeld's apprentice.

I went in to say one last good-bye to Dr. Lansfeld, who was now on the step-down unit and progressing well. I was transferring off his service and heading across town to a world-renowned arrhythmia clinic before I graduated. When I walked in, a welcoming smile crossed his face as he put down the book he was reading on the night stand. It was Anne Harrington's book *The Cure Within*, and he set it right next to a dog-eared copy of *The Lost Art of Healing*.

"Dr. Bauman, much as I am sure you can't believe this, I'm going to miss you," Dr. Lansfeld began. "So much so, and with the ulterior motive of hopefully working with you in the future on research in placebo and the healing effects of the mind in cardiac surgery, that I have talked to some of my friends at Brigham and Women's Hospital. They want to interview you for one of their two cardiology fellowship positions. Given that I told them you were one of the most gifted residents I have had the privilege of working with, I think you have a good shot at getting it."

"Dr. Lansfeld, I don't know what to say."

"I also have one more surprise, from both Billy and me," he said. Reaching down by his bedside, he pulled up Sir Luke Fildes's painting of *The Doctor*. Inscribed on the bottom were the words:

The science is crucial, but the art heals the soul. Never forget the art!
                —Hartley Lansfeld, M.D.

JUNG'S LAMENT

"Everywhere I go I find a poet has been there before me."
—**Sigmund Freud**

THE CRACK OF the cover closing on the huge tome could be heard throughout the house. This was not the first time Jung's *Red Book* had pushed my apparently limited comprehension to the brink.

"I don't understand this damn thing," I said with a clear note of irritation to no one in particular.

"You are not supposed to" came the audible, deep-throated reply.

Startled, I looked quickly at the doorway of the study to see if my son had come in while I was working—the voice had clearly sounded male. But except for my dog beside me, I was alone. I shut my eyes to focus within, thinking it was nothing but a strong inner thought. I was little relieved with this interpretation since its coming from without had seemed so definite, so autonomous, so other....

My feeling of falling was as if I were riding on a roller coaster, my stomach turning topsy-turvy as I went over the edge and dropped. This falling seemed to last minutes, until abruptly I landed on my feet and the sight of stone buildings came powerfully into focus in front of me. The stone gave the look of a 16th-century castle: gray, large, and imposing. As I entered through the open, massive wooden door, two bookend fireplaces came to view, cutting into the columns and defining a grotto-like space. I moved closer and saw a lectern with parchment paper, a quill pen, and a copy of Jung's autobiography, *Memories, Dreams, Reflections*, resting on top. The book was well worn, as if it had been read and studied over and over again. Suddenly I sensed a presence; behind me approached the great man himself. Aghast, I realized that within my waking imaginal world, I had gained access to C. G. Jung's vacation home in Bollingen. Groping for my intellectual bearings, I heard the same deep-throated voice saying, "Approach us as if we are real and listen attentively to what we say" (Jung, 1973a, p. 181).

Dr. Jung took a seat on the raised stone hearth and began stirring his midday meal, cooking slowly in a cast iron pot over the fire. He stared into the flames as if deep in thought, his only acknowledgment of me a wave of his left hand toward an unadorned wooden chair, an apparent invitation to sit. I sat down beside him, our knees almost touching. He had the look of a simple peasant man, living contentedly in his primitive dwelling, lost forever in the Middle Ages. He was still wearing his wide-brimmed straw hat from a morning of chopping kindling, his sleeves rolled up, and his ever-present pipe lodged securely in the left corner of his mouth. Finally, while still staring straight ahead, as if talking to no one but the kettle in front of him, he spoke.

"*Liber Novus* is not about intellectual understanding!" These words hung in the air for minutes, heavy between us. I was about to ask him to elaborate when he raised his left hand again, this time for silence. He turned and faced me, his hand on his forehead, his eyes closed, his words emerging slowly and powerfully from deep within. "It is a book about how to live life, about how to be in relationship with your soul. It is for the everyday person and everyday therapist. If it has any redeeming value for this time, it is because it is a method, a how-to for allowing the other to have voice. This is my lament! I am now the dead that I spoke of in *The Red Book*, and the answers to the unanswered questions of the dead must be found."

I shifted uncomfortably in my chair, for a moment losing my connection to the fantasy, my conscious cramp questioning the legitimacy of what was occurring. I just as quickly caught myself, remembering Jung's earlier "as-if" admonition and entered the dialogue for the first time: "Dr. Jung, I am moved by the urgency of your lament and would be honored to discuss these questions with you in more depth."

Jung's eyes narrowed, and with a stare that seemed to be judging the sincerity of my intent, took an extra-long pull on his pipe before nodding his assent. "When I was in my confrontation with the unconscious and seeking my lost soul, I became aware of the spirit of the times. This is the way of rationality, causality, and scientism. These were strong when I lived and even stronger now. You have been caught by this spirit as was I, and this is very dangerous, for it can choke out any voice of the soul and the spirit of the depths. Now in its grip, therapy has become a series of precisely plotted maps: cognitive and behavioral, causal and reductive, measured, evidence-based, and manualized, as if the soul could be caught in a step-by-step cookbook."

"I too bemoan this turn of the times," I sadly replied, but also noticed a sense of excitement to enter a discussion on a topic that had affected me for years. "I see it every day in my psychiatric practice and find I can often get caught in the security of the current striving for algorithms to fit every generalized case and symptom. Though I can understand why this turn toward treatment as something common and measured would disturb you, I am struck that this was an issue you never shied away from in your life's work. You were always the champion of the individual and the irrational. Help me to understand how this is now your lament."

"Gladly," Jung replied. "I had a different task in my lifetime. The questions from the dead that preoccupied my work were the problems of the opposites and the shadow side of God. But I was allowed to know in my life that I had completed my task when at that moment in my sailboat, 'on the Obersee,…my father appeared and patted my shoulder saying, You have done it rightly, I thank you.' This was my happiest moment, for I knew I had answered his unresolved question (Jung, 2010, p. ix, fn. 5).

"But now a deep aspect of my unanswered work haunts me and comes to haunt you and all who would listen and feel the soul's yearning. The declaration she made, that I fought so strongly not to hear, yet

still echoes after these many years: that inner voice of a woman saying, 'What you are doing is art' (Jung, 1973a, p. 185). I hated this and
called her names. I went a different direction, that of science and em-
piricism, probably necessary in that epoch, but came to believe late in
my life that she may have been right all along."

"I always understood, from your comments on that event, that the
concern was about her inflating you and leading you off on a wild
goose chase of becoming a painter in Paris," I said quickly.

A deep, resounding belly laugh filled the hearth room as my last
comment had clearly touched Jung's famous sense of humor. "Ah, yes,
my painting fantasies!" he said with the hint of laughter still playing
through his words. "I was quite full of it back then, and needed to set
her straight about not taking me down that road. But, you see, I didn't
continue in the way I truly believed. I took her literally about what
qualified as art and what I thought were her implications, and then
defensively diagnosed her and turned away. I didn't push her further.
I didn't continue the conversation once I had a stable position of my
own from which to speak. I gave no quarter in allowing her voice and
character to emerge."

Jung paused, taking a long, reflective pull on his pipe, and said,
"Now I understand her to mean something very different, that possibly what I was doing in *Liber Novus* was a new method, closer to art
than to science—something that Herbert Read had been trying to
convince me of for years. In our exchange of letters shortly before I
died, I realized 'that the great dream is always spoken through the
artist as a mouthpiece' and that true artists have learned 'to be objective with their own psyche. They have learned to discriminate between
the thing that you do and the thing that happens to you' (Jung, 1975,
p. 591). This is the key to *The Red Book*, the realization that the soul is
alive and has her own voice. Let's have our discussion concentrate on
this: the method and the ways of discriminating her voice. This is what
I believe is lost in our everyday world and in our usual therapeutic en-
deavors, and it is a change in this attitude that is her greatest desire."

Jung slowly rose from his seat at the hearth, reaching down to ladle ample portions of stew for us both. "Come join me on the loggia for lunch. It is a beautiful day by the lake and a great place to continue our discussion." As we carried the hand-hewed wooden bowls filled with a venison stew toward our outdoor seating, Jung asked that I go to his wine stock and procure a bottle of the Tuscan red. "It will complement the venison nicely and also invite Dionysus, who may open our dialogue to even richer veins."

We sat staring at the lapping waves of the Zürichsee, its probing fingers reaching ever closer on the rocky shores in front of us. We had both finished our stew and were now pouring our second glass of wine when Jung continued, "Do you understand why I want to focus solely on method?" I quickly shook my head that I did not. "Because we are all suffering from this infernal need to know everything, to think we must have explanations," Jung answered briskly.

Excited by these thoughts, I jumped in, saying, "That reminds me of the poet W. H. Auden and a line from one of his poems: 'We are lived by powers we pretend to understand'" (cited in Hillman & Shamdasani, 2013, p. 228).

"*Ja, ja*, that is exactly it!" Jung responded, his voice rising. "All the theories of psychology, mine included, concentrate on projection and integration of these projections and therefore move too quickly 'from the experience of [personified] figures to explanatory principles.' One needs to linger 'with the experience of the figures.' This is what the poets do and then 'the gradual reabsorption and disappearance of the figures' is no longer the goal" (Watkins, 2000, p. 79).

Jung paused with this last sentence, his gaze turning quickly away. For just a moment I imagined a look in his eyes as if a feeling of remorse had come upon him. After some minutes staring toward the block of stone that he had meticulously carved to help deal with the grief of his wife's death, he slowly turned back toward me, his face softened, his voice quieting as he spoke. "I once commented that as an individual integrates the anima, the anima then becomes a function and no longer a personified figure (Hillman, 1985, pp. 115–116). I regret those words now. That was an act of intellectual hubris and only helped to reinforce the ego's power position in current psychological theory. I am not sure how, in all my years of creating theory, I could have been so callous toward the soul, as I knew that the process of personification occurs spontaneously in the psyche. 'It is not we who personify them, but they [the personified figures] have a personal nature from the very beginning' (Jung, 1967, p. 42). This point is important for our discussion of method. *The Red Book* is filled with spontaneous personifications and automatically creates a dialogical practice. I can feel emotions toward the figures as they arise, and theirs toward me. I can love them and hate them, but I cannot remain indifferent to them. The 'little people of the soul' will not allow us this luxury. Miguel de Unamuno said it best: 'In order to love everything, in order to pity everything, human and extra-human, living and non-living, you must feel everything within yourself, you must personalize everything. For everything that it loves, everything that it pities, love personalizes'" (cited in Hillman, 1975, p. 15).

Suddenly Jung stood, his glass of wine still in hand, and began pacing with an increased vigor to step and voice. "Through Philemon I learned that the 'I' does not create the figures or characters of the soul, but it is just one figure in the house of psyche (Jung, 1973a, p. 183). This then moves away from theories oriented to a 'goal of strengthening the ego and its gradual assimilation of other portions of the psyche' (Watkins, 2000, p. 122). Instead, the 'I' becomes a character herself and can be observed by the other imaginal figures of the soul and more importantly enter a relationship with these figures. The new goal is not strength and dominion but an 'increasing dialogue and articulation of self and other' (Watkins, 2000, p. 105). I cannot say this more passionately: 'Theory must conform to experience rather than the other way around' (Watkins, 2000, p. 102). We need a therapeutic method which encourages phenomenology and the engagement of the imaginal figures 'in the manner they present themselves'" (Watkins, 2000, p. 102).

"Dr. Jung," I said, matching his ardor. "I cannot agree more with the passionate position you are taking in regard to method and the autonomy of character. I would love to add some of my thoughts and experiences to our discussion." Jung nodded his welcome.

"First, to go back to figures and their independence," I began. "I think that what you showed in *The Red Book* was that characters come unbidden and, when allowed, have a voice and position outside the 'I.' Also, your comments regarding their personal nature are perfectly clear from the beginning that it is not the 'I' that personifies them as a technique of therapy. This, in my opinion, makes what you were pursuing in *The Red Book* closer to great fiction and therefore art. Fiction writers report many anecdotes about the sovereignty of the characters occurring in their novels and short stories. Psychologist Mary Watkins has written about this in her brilliant book *Invisible Guests*. For instance, she quotes Elizabeth Bowen as saying, 'The term "creation of a character" (or characters) is misleading. Characters preexist, they are found.... One cannot "make" characters, only marionettes' (cited in Watkins, 2000, pp. 93–94). And the poet Wallace Stevens says, in *Credences of Summer,* 'The characters speak because they want to speak...free for a moment' (cited in Watkins, 2000, p. 93). Or how about Dostoevsky commenting to friends on Ivan's character in *The Brothers Karamazov.* The characters' 'arguments can arise independently of the author's desires' (cited in Watkins, 2000, p. 96). And lastly, one that will be close to your heart, Goethe saying, 'The songs made me, not I them'" (cited in Watkins, 2000, p. 94).

Another booming laugh echoed across the lake as Jung replied, "Yes, you knew I would love that statement from Johann Wolfgang von Goethe, my great-grandfather, or so the family legend says. But also I am delighted with these writers' personal stories and the connection to fiction. I was always strongly drawn to *Faust* and can easily see my same experiences reflected in these quotes. I never knew who would spontaneously arise in *Liber Novus* and was often shocked with what they said or asked of me, similar to Dostoevsky's understanding. It is also beginning to make sense how both you and my soul could believe *The Red Book* truly was art. I notice now a statement coming to my mind from years ago, that the 'main value of a work of art does not lie in its causal development but in its living effect upon ourselves' (Jung, 1960, p. 183). The effect on me of *Liber Novus* set the course for the rest of my life. But please say more of your thoughts and reflections. I am intrigued."

"I would like to go further into our discussion of therapy as fiction and art, going along with your view that the psyche is involved in mythopoesis, the constant making of stories. I believe one of your great discoveries was that 'myth or story is basic' (cited in Hillman & Shamdasani, 2013, p. 64) and that it is most usefully conveyed not through abstraction or generalization or summary or analysis or interpretation—all criteria making not only for a poor story but for poor therapy as well. Instead, it is best told through the sensual encounter with characters whose presence comes alive by meeting them in our moment-to-moment senses."

"I remember an example of this from when I was writing *Liber Secundus*," Jung remarked. "I was going into the castle of the old man locked away with his books. I had asked for lodging for the night and had just begun to settle in when suddenly his daughter entered my room, pale and comely. I was sure this was a banal fairy tale emerging out of me. I was irritated and not believing that any of this was real, but just some 'hackneyed nonsense...[of] empty fantasies...[and] the sorriest likeness to those foolishly threadbare scenes in novels' (Jung, 2009, pp. 261–262). But she screamed at me, 'You wretch, how can you doubt that I am real?' (Jung, 2009, p. 262). I began to awake to her longing, going deeply into the sensual experiences I was having: tightening chest, grabbing throat, as if a feeling of pity; a shard of light across her face, a turn toward me with beaming smile and a sense that beauty and purity had entered my world. She had come to life in reality and I could doubt no more."

"Dr. Jung, I am profoundly touched by your description of this memory and found myself carried by your words into her presence. In my opinion this was art, for 'all art objects are sensuous and are produced by a process that is sensuous and not logical. Art begins when we surrender ourselves to this world of images and their autonomy'

(Burroway, 2007, p. 4). The people we work with in therapy are 'actually sensual objects and as we create this work of art we do it within the sensual experience of the character, by getting inside the character' (Olen Butler, 2001). There is an old saying: 'God is in the details. Let's substitute: the human condition resides in the details, the sense details'" (Olen Butler, 2005, p. 14).

"*Ja*," Jung replied, his head nodding, his eyes partially closed as if our discussion had taken him reflectively inward. "You are saying that when we have a 'loving and curious stance toward our experiences' (Mindell, 1993, p. 85) and stay close to the sensory details, then the soul comes alive and therapy becomes art. Yes, this was my experience in *The Red Book*, over and over again. My conscious cramp was strong at first, but as it melted, this was surely what occurred. But now you are saying that this can happen in our daily routine, that there is a way to have this experience with yourself and your patients. I also believe this, a way to do active imagination all the time. Everyone with their own *Red Book*, dreaming the dream onward, and moving toward my greatest yearning—*esse in anima*—to be in soul."

Jung stretched his back and, slowly rising from his chair, said, "This has been a stimulating experience speaking with you and could be described most succinctly by one of the great words of my native tongue, *betrachten*. It means to consider and to be made pregnant by (Humbert, 1984, p. 10). I believe we have considered much today, and I for one am pregnant with the ideas and emotions constellated by our discussion. But I am tired now and even though I am dead, the dead still tire," Jung said with one last hearty laugh. "I will have to explain that little-known fact to you at another time, but please come back tomorrow; there is still much for us to explore."

Suddenly I was alert and in my study, my dog still sleeping soundly beside me. A deep breath came audibly pouring from my mouth and a sense of mental and physical exhaustion coursed through my body. But even with the fatigue, a smile crossed my lips. I thought of our wonderful dialogue and pulled my chair up to the computer to begin its transcription, not wanting to take a chance of forgetting anything that had taken place. I would rest for the night and, as Jung requested, enter imaginal reality again tomorrow.

☙

I awoke late on a crisp, blue-sky Saturday morning, having stayed at my computer until the day's final hour, trying to squeeze out every last word from my fantasied Bollingen visit. A vivid dream had been my alarm to the day, but before I had a chance to write it down, my dog's pleading eyes caught my gaze, imploring me to tend to her daily constitutional. We set out on our favorite forest path, the yellowed and rust-colored fall leaves crackling beneath our feet, as she enjoyed every compelling smell, and I enjoyed musing about yesterday's conversation with Dr. Jung.

The familiar "ding" of my iPhone pulled me quickly from my reverie to the incoming text message from my wife. She was already at work, taking pictures of newborns at the local hospital, and just saying good morning with a smiling, heart-eyed emoji and a copy of the weekend "honey do" list following close behind. Realizing I wanted to make the crossover to the world of fantasy before starting the chores, I gave a firm tug on my dog's collar and turned a clearly disappointed girl toward home.

Sitting in the study cross-legged on my zafu, slowly breathing in deep, relaxing, meditative breaths, I tried to hold the image in my mind's eye of Jung's vacation home and the massive wooden door through which I had entered so easily just the day before. But I was losing to the countercurrent of wandering focus and the building frustrations that became evident in a tightening back and stiffening shoulders.

"Damn," I said, realizing that none of the usual entry methods into the world of imagination would be of any benefit today. But I knew I had other ways in, though I didn't like to use them unless necessary. I seemed to use a body channel, as Jung might have classified me and as he described in his 1916 paper "The Transcendent Function" (Jung, 1969, p. 84). It was in this paper that he first began to write about a therapy style he was later to call "active imagination." He already was hinting at different channels for accessing the unconscious, depending on a patient's talents and disposition. He referred to the three types of channels *visual, audio-verbal,* and *body,* and also suggested entering proprioceptively through clay modeling or other forms of sculpting. I had always loved this essay as well as his earlier, less quoted one, "Association, Dream and Hysterical Symptom." In both papers he shows the beginnings of his later thinking on how the soul is alive in the moment through body, mood, and image (Jung, 1973b, pp. 353–407). I was hoping to speak with Jung later about my intuitions regarding these early writings and how they might apply to our thoughts late in yesterday's conversation about active imagination being available all the time.

But first I had to find a way into his world, and the body channel had never failed to provide a quick entry to the imaginal. My hesitancy was often how strong, overwhelming, and sometimes frightening this path could be for me. I had been experimenting for years with various body techniques, including Mary Whitehouse's authentic movement and the Kalahari dance methods for altering consciousness (Keeney, 2010), but no matter how often I used them, they still packed a power of the numinous that was quite shocking. Either of these, or other body techniques, could be choices today, but instead I decided to follow a recent dream. *In it I was whirling like a top, and began to see visions of a small native man leading me into the woods.* I was somewhat familiar with the legend of how Rumi discovered the whirling dervish method, and I decided to try this practice in my office.

I got up from my meditation pillow and moved to the center of the room. I placed one arm over my head with the other extended outward as I began turning clockwise in a tight circle with my left foot stable as a pivot for balance. My eyes slightly open, I spun, slowly at first and then a bit faster until the room started to blur. All at once what looked like a large V cutting into gray concrete came into view. I lay down on the floor to stop the dizziness, my attention now pinpointed on this letter; suddenly the words of a sentence followed and drew sharply into focus.

VOCATUS.ATQUE.NON VOCATUS.DEUS.ADERIT. I was at the entrance to Jung's family home on the Seestrasse in Küsnacht, staring at the famous Latin saying carved above his front door, its English translation coming instantly to mind: "Called or not called, God will be there." I took a breath, gathered myself, and knocked, hearing the scrape of a chair and the creak of floorboards as someone rose and moved slowly toward the door.

"Ah, it is you," Jung said, clearly happy to see me. "I was hoping you would arrive today. Come, the garden will be the perfect spot to continue our conversation, and expecting you, I already placed a pitcher of lemonade there for us to enjoy." I followed behind as we walked around the right corner of his home leading toward the garden and its magnificent view of the lake. Coming into sight as well was his beloved sailboat, tethered in the harbor area beside the boathouse, rocking gently with the waves. Jung noticed the direction of my gaze and said, "I have already been out for a morning sail, but maybe we shall go again later."

We sat at a small table Jung had set up on the circular terrace in the upper garden, partially shaded by a young and spreading elm tree. We both arranged our chairs so that the snowcapped Alps were easily visible across the lake. I poured our drinks and we sat quietly for a moment, reverent of the beauty, before Jung began to speak.

"As I was looking at the mountains and their reflection on the water, I began thinking of sailing and its wonderments. Nothing is better for the practice of opening oneself to the rhythm of the spirit, to *geschenlassen*—or in English, to let happen (Humbert, 1984, p. 9). This is so hard for modern people, even more now than when I was alive." He softly chuckled as he remembered something. I waited. "I used to test people in my office on this very thing," he said, "when they first came to see me. I smoked my pipe most days, and before a new patient would come into my study for the consultation, I would put 'a still smoldering match from the lighting of my pipe into the small antique bronze mortar I used for an ashtray.' There in the mortar would also be the tiniest bit of paper, and suddenly a match 'could flare up again and consume everything in the vessel. Anyone who solicitously tried to blow out the little conflagration was gravely rebuked. Don't interfere!' I would say (Jaffé, 1984, pp. 102–103).

"It was here I had my chance to teach my patients about *geschenlassen*. How is it they first could not just give it attention, consideration, or as I called it yesterday, *betrachten*? To just let it happen as long as there was no immediate danger? How did they know 'that life may not know better than the correcting mind'? I tried to instruct my patients that the 'aim was to understand the hidden intentions of the organizer and to penetrate its secrets' (Jaffé, 1984, p. 102–103), that life may know better, that one needed to consider the hidden intentions of the organizer and, if not interfered with, where they might flow."

Jung's words echoed throughout my mind. Then, with a sudden spark of realization, I said, "This is the key, isn't it, Dr. Jung, to what you discovered and practiced in *The Red Book*? You took whatever arose, you operated with it. You gave it your special attention, concentrated on it, and observed its changes objectively. You spared no effort to this task and devoted yourself to the soul and her ways. You questioned her, had it out with her, tried to come to terms with her, no matter how she showed herself in fantasy. You did this carefully and attentively. But even more than this, you disciplined yourself and didn't allow anything in that did not belong. You didn't diagnose her and call her reductive names from a diagnostic and statistical manual, or revert to childhood dynamics or to biological formulations. For in the end you had the courage to believe that 'the fantasy-image has everything it needs'" (Jung, 1970, p. 526).

"*Ja*, what you say is true and you say it so beautifully," Jung replied with a tone of appreciation. "I can hear that my lament is becoming ever clearer to you, as this way of being with the soul is sadly fading, even in so-called Jungian circles. It is barely heard of, otherwise taught, in most current schools of psychology. In much of the Jungian training around the world, a patient must jump through innumerable hoops of development before this method is considered ethical in its recommendation. But I remember from yesterday that we both thought there was a way to a *Red Book* for everyone. Tell me more of your ideas in this vein."

"Well," I began eagerly, "first I would start with the current dream research that shows we are actually dreaming all the time, 24 hours a day. In fact, one of your Jungian students, Arnold Mindell, calls this sub-terranean flow 'the dreaming' and connects it to both the wave function in quantum physics and to ancient aboriginal mythical beliefs."

"That is quite fascinating," Jung replied. "It hadn't yet been proven in my lifetime that the dream world was available in other mediums than in dreams of the night. It is also validating to see some of my in-tuitions about physics, which I would discuss with Pauli, now begin-ning to bear fruit. It was clear to me even then that, in any period of *abaissement du niveau mental*, or the lowering of consciousness, the world of fantasy and dream could break through. I maintained that while awake one could allow the soul to speak through free associa-tion and active imagination (Humbert, 1984, p. 15). However, I like this idea of calling the ever-moving, constantly creative lava flow of the col-lective unconscious 'the dreaming.' This naming would more readily imply that all therapy is 'the stuff of dreams,' and accessing the dream-ing world, the goal. Also, wasn't Mindell a student of my nephew, Franz Riklin, Jr.?"

"Yes, he was."

"Ah, not a surprise, then, that with Franz as his mentor he would think in this way. Franz always had a foot in the other world, some-times both feet, but he never failed to bring back the most amazing things. I remember one time watching him work after I had died. A woman had been brought to see him by the psychiatric emergency group, as she was in a catatonic stupor and couldn't talk or move. That was in a time mostly before medication, and as a psychiatrist he occasionally saw patients like this in his office. She was completely mute and therefore he had no verbal way to make contact with her. Instead, going deep within himself he connected to the dream world, or what I might have called the 'psychoid level of the unconscious.' There he saw her dead husband banging on his office window, saying his final good-bye. The banging was so loud and caused such a racket that it could even be heard in the waiting room by his next patient. Suddenly, the woman came out of her catatonic state and ran from the office, quite thrilled and screaming happily" (Mindell, 2013, p. 63).

Barely able to contain my rising excitement, I asserted, "Dr. Jung, this is just what I meant earlier by taking whatever arises and working with it. Dr. Riklin could not enter through the typical verbal or auditory method of most conventional therapies, so he followed what was the strongest signal for him in that moment, which was an inner feeling. Not letting anything else in, and concentrating on this feeling, it spontaneously transformed into a vision. This is the method that we spoke of yesterday and the new way of discriminating the soul's voice. In my opinion, it lies in realizing that therapists are sensualists, and if they follow what is happening with careful awareness through the bare bones of their sensory channels and do not leave prematurely for interpretation or explanation, then figures begin to be discovered, arising in the conduits of the soul's choosing: visual, auditory, proprioceptive, kinesthetic, countertransference (which could be called the relationship channel), and lastly the world, as synchronicities" (Mindell, 2000).

"*Ach, so,*" said Jung. "I was gifted in my life, as is evidenced in *The Red Book*, by working with this 'dreaming,' as you call it, in a mostly visual and verbal way, but many others must enter through a different route. This I can easily believe, as so many patients and therapists get caught in the intellect, and the work never takes on the quality of the numinous. But what I also see is that you are adding a precision to the work: by giving scrupulous and methodical attention to where the libido is flowing, figures begin to awaken. As I said during my alchemical studies many years ago, you could start with any of these aspects of the *prima materia*: 'a spontaneous fantasy, a dream, an irrational mood, an affect' (Jung, 1970, p. 526). However, now we are saying: Take any one of these, but stay aware of the sensory channel in which they occur and start there, then follow with exactness and it will lead to the soul.

"This makes me rethink some of my case memories and how I was doing much of what we are now describing through my intuition,"

Jung continued. "In fact, some current-day Jungian analysts write off many of my therapy successes to what they believe is my great but un-teachable intuition. Now, however, we are imagining that it may have been trainable all along, through a rigorous practice of awareness that focuses on the flow of sensual energy."

Jung smiled to himself for a moment, caught in a remembrance of a case from years past. "She came to see me on referral for a one-time consultation—a young school teacher who had traveled a great dis-tance from her village in the Canton Solothurn. She suffered from al-most complete insomnia and also terribly from the feeling of not meeting the demands of life. I asked her to find some means of relaxa-tion, but I could see from her face she did not understand. I told her of my sailing on the lake, and of letting myself go with the wind, but again her eyes said no to my suggestions. I was saddened; I so wanted to help with only this one meeting together. Then, as I talked of sailing and of the wind, I heard the voice of my mother singing a lullaby to my little sister, as she used to do when I was eight or nine, a story of a little girl, on a little boat, on the Rhine, with little fishes. And I began, almost without doing it on purpose, to hum what I was telling her about the wind, the waves, the sailing, and relaxation to the tune of the little lullaby. I hummed those sensations and I could see she was enchant-ed. Years later I met her referring physician at a conference, who told me that her insomnia had been cured during this one visit, never to return" (Jaffé, 1984, pp. 106–107).

"What a lovely story, Dr. Jung. It is a wonderful example of what we have been saying about awareness and the senses. You followed her facial feedback and the clues in her eyes, noticing that with the inter-vention you were providing, there was no connection to her psyche. You did not interpret resistance, but were open to trusting what was happening, to *geschenlassen*. Now you responded with careful con-sideration, *betrachten*, by assiduously following the spontaneous aris-ing of the auditory channel in the voice of your mother and the lullaby. You allowed yourself to be thrown into the moving river of psychic energy. You didn't stop and stand on the riverbank of explanation and speak about the lacunae of her mother complex or a missing self-soothing object, but instead picked up the rocking of the waves in your body and the humming of the song. It was then that the soul came alive as the archetypal comforting mother flowed through you, not interpreted by you, and the little girl in her was cured."

"Your analysis of what took place in this case is quite fascinating," Jung said. "I can see how this is an important addition to my method and allows the soul more room to communicate in whatever way she is choosing. It would be exciting to do this work in person. Do you think you might have a dream we could work with?"

"It just so happens," I said, surprised, "that after our penetrating discussion yesterday, I awoke with the most unusual dream but without any chance yet for reflection."

"Please, tell the dream," Jung said.

I am in a house with an unknown woman of foreign descent, perhaps Eastern European. She is showing me a silver dinner knife. It had the name Igor Petrokovic engraved on it. I awoke perplexed, with no real sense as to any personal associations. I did tell my wife the dream and made an unconscious slip and said 'ego' instead of 'Igor' when recalling the name," I said, chuckling.

Jung enjoyed a robust laugh himself over my comment, and gazing at his uninhibited, childlike enjoyment, I remembered reading about how he had been adamant in his teaching that a therapist must have and allow all his or her emotions to be present when working on a dream. "Well, that gives us a good start, *ja*?" he said, with a titter still in his voice. "It most definitely has to do with your current ego being sacrificed to something greater, to the silver, the metal of the soul, very powerful, very important. Our discussion of the soul's lament has touched you deeply."

As Dr. Jung was making his comments about the imagery, I noticed the slightest changes occurring in my body—a mild tightening of my throat, as if sadness were about to visit...a quickly passing feeling of dizziness, so fleeting I could have easily denied its existence. Observing the change in my focus, Jung commented, "I see you are noticing something other than my continued work with the images and symbols. I would typically go on with associations and believe that the touch of emotion you are experiencing was a positive aha that indicates we are on the right track. But I think this is the moment, as you might say, that the soul is beginning to emerge in a different channel" (Mindell, 2001).

I nodded my agreement, trying to keep some attention on the tiniest "flirts"—Mindell's term for whatever catches one's attention—now attempting to come to life. "Dr. Jung," I said, "Let's follow these diminutive signals and not talk any longer at this moment." Jung nodded his acceptance. I stood to follow more closely the strongest and yet evanescent feelings of dizziness. I had done this many times in the past and knew I had to slowly amplify or increase the signals in the channel in which they were occurring. Because it was both proprioceptive (a body sensation) and also a sense of movement (kinesthetic channel), I decided to focus on the movement and see where it might take me. I shut my eyes to eliminate visual aspects of self because the visual channel was closest to my primary identity, which, according to the dream, was being sacrificed. This was also the reason for cutting off the audio-verbal channel earlier: it would prevent a complete entering into the language the soul was choosing for communication, which at this moment was the body. As I did this, I noticed the same dizziness, now increasing, and a feeling of being pulled or pushed to the right. I followed this pulling with increased focus and attention, when suddenly I was thrown to the ground. Jung was quickly on his feet to see if I was all right, but I silently waved him off and continued, now quite caught in the aliveness of the imagination.

I was down on my knees now, feeling the concrete of the terrace beneath me, my body wracked with an overwhelming sense of sadness and loneliness and plaintive sobbing, and yet, amazingly, it didn't feel like my tears or my sadness. It was as if another was having me feel his pain. I began to crawl from my position, noticing immediately my crumpled body, as though my right leg were dragging from paralysis, right arm crippled, right facies contorted. I took up more consciously these body positions and slowly it became clear that a figure was emerging through me. He moved me toward Jung and began to rub "his" head on Jung's leg while the garbled word *slow* came from my mouth over and over again.

For a moment I came out of my reverie and looked up at Dr. Jung. He was rubbing my head and tears had come to his eyes. He spoke, not to me, but to the other in me. "I see that you have finally come to this man, and I cry with tears of joy and sadness for your arrival—the sadness for your suffering from being ostracized for so long, the joy that you can finally be welcomed as other and your voice heard." We sat for what seemed minutes, Jung on the concrete bench surrounding the terrace, me on the ground in front of him, all the while he continued to rub my head as an inconsolable longing remained my companion.

Finally, as I got up and returned to my chair and Dr. Jung moved to his previous and more comfortable seat, he was the first to find words. "I was deeply moved by your work and glad we were able to experience the dream together in this way or I wouldn't have believed the numinosity possible with these methods." Jung reached for his pipe on the bench beside him and in an unconscious ritual that he had performed thousands of times, tapped out his finished ashes and filled the bowl with tobacco. Then as he blew the smoke from its lighting, he turned toward me with a voice sounding of seriousness and admonition: "No matter that we have found other ways for the soul to commune with us, two things of old now become paramount: ethics and the *auseinandersetzung.*

"First on ethics, as this takes front and center. It will be easy to go back to your everyday life and ego. For though your work was powerful, alive, and very real, unless you ethically form an ongoing relationship with the figure that came to you, it will have all been for nothing. It will drop from site as if a momentary wave in the ocean. It is one thing to bring the soul forward, it is another to follow its calling. Without that commitment, all is just power (Jung, 1973a, pp. 192–193).

"Second, we have spoken much about letting it happen, and of considering and making pregnant," Jung continued. "Both of these were on great display in your recent dream work. But now, as I learned in *The Red Book*, comes the third thing, maybe the most important of all, the *auseinandersetzung*, or to confront oneself (Humbert, 1984, p. 12). You see, he is here, this man of yours, and you feel him in your body. Keep getting to know him, but also confront him and push him. Give him life through drawing him with pencil and paints or, in your case, molding him with clay or sculpture, for he needs your earth to stay real. But remember this last advice, for I learned it the hard way: A conversation is inevitable because he demands it; that is, if you don't want to just surrender unconditionally to him. Speak with him, ask him about his longing and sadness, stay close to him, because you now know and feel that he is an independent personality and you cannot expect that he will accept your standpoint without further ado. To not do this would be to flee and choose not to come to a deeper relationship and understanding" (Jung, 2009, pp. 260–261).

A deep sigh escaped from my lips as the feeling of longing from my inner companion continued to linger. I tried to take one more breath to relax before looking over at Dr. Jung. "This was a day I did not expect," I said. "I thought we might talk further of art and theory and ideas, but instead they came alive and became very real, like independent souls in my psyche. I am very tired now, though not dead!" Jung smiled at my play on his words from the end of our time together yesterday.

"It seems as though we have come to the end of our conversation, at least for the present time," Jung responded. "I want to say that I am happy you've had this experience. I am speaking of the feeling realization of the reality of the psyche. It is one that is crucial and in the end, sadly, one that very few people have, even therapists! *The Red Book* taught me this. My experience there showed me that I must 'take seriously every unknown wanderer who personally inhabits the inner world, since they are real because they are effectual.' In the end, the real is what works (Jung, 2009, p. 260, 260 fn. 15). I am glad to have taught you this and that you heard the soul's yearning, her longing to be taken seriously." I mouthed a humble thank-you.

Jung smiled and continued, "You also heard my lament and through our discussions reconnected me to the alchemists, the deepest roots of my work. I can hear them saying, 'What nature leaves imperfect, the art perfects' (Jung, 1973a, p. 255). Now I understand what the soul was saying to me so many years ago. She was not looking for the literal, scientific truth, as I was, but her 'interest was in finding the artistic truth. Her intent was to reshape the literal truth of the world into forms that reveal the deeper, universal truths of our existence'" (Olen Butler, 2001). This is art!

Jung slowly lifted himself from his chair. I stood next to him, ready to shake his hand good-bye, but surprisingly he reached out and patted my shoulder, saying, "I can now do as my father did long ago: I can pat your shoulder and say, 'Thank you,' for I know today there are many trying to answer the questions rightly."

THERAPY AND THE ACT OF CHARACTERIZATION

How could I have started so late? What was I thinking? I had lived in Chicago my whole life and knew well its Friday afternoons and rush hour traffic. I must always leave the office by 4 p.m.; if not, I'm sure to become part of the modern day torture we naively call the "drive home from work." My last patient had been a squeezed-into-the-schedule emergency by our office manager. She had called begging to see me earlier than her regular appointment, and I knew if I didn't accommodate her, most likely she would spend the weekend cutting herself and feeling suicidal. But by acquiescing, had I placed the therapy on a regressive course? I had just started sessions with her and was already having countertransference issues. I wondered what my Kohutian colleagues at the University of Chicago would think about the frame. And what about my new office mate at the university, who called himself a Kernbergian? He had already implied in our peer supervision, not too subtly I might add, that I was lax in addressing the negative transference. I took a long breath and distinctly heard my wife's voice questioning my decision two years ago when offered the position.

"You will be like the proverbial 'fish out of water,'" I could still hear her saying. "You think differently with your Jungian training. It's not good for you to put yourself in these theoretical-adversarial situations all the time. I remember well what they do to you."

I had overruled her and not given much credence to her feelings. I remember commenting, "This is not the same as Milwaukee, or even the Jung Institute where I struggled with rigid viewpoints. I'm different now. I have had much analysis and can handle myself with the various theories and opinions. Anyway, they are offering such a good salary and benefits. We can't pass this up."

Now sitting in traffic, moving glacially along Lake Shore Drive, I thought she might have been right all along. A glance at the car clock brought me abruptly back to the present and why I was irritated for getting a late start. I was on my way to hear Dr. William McIntyre, M.D., give a lecture at the Jung Institute in Evanston. It had been thirty years since I had first come to see him during the initial year of my psychiatric residency. I made the drive down from Milwaukee for four years for our one-and-a-half-hour sessions every Tuesday. I still considered these the most important four years of my life. He had helped me through nightmarish dreams and the terrible panic and inferiority that were their accompaniment. Now, as I glanced both at the brochure advertising his lecture on "Therapy and the Act of Characterization" at 5 p.m. and at the car clock that read 5:10 p.m., I could only shake my head. I had been looking forward to this night for months, as a chance to see Bill again and as a reprieve from the overintellectualized halls of academic life. Here I was, stuck in traffic, about to miss it. I could only hope to make it for the question-and-answer dialogues that followed the formal presentation and were always quite rousing. I was sure tonight's would not disappoint, since Dr. McIntyre had just published a controversial new book questioning the omniscient role of the analyst as interpreter of the unconscious, and instead was advocating the role of what he was calling the "histor." The histor, as I was coming to understand it from his writings, seeks to "find out the truth" from various characters. She is "the narrator as inquirer, constructing a narrative" (Scholes & Kellogg, 1966, cited in Watkins, 2000, p. 125, fn. 27). This allowed the figures or characters to become and remain more autonomous. Or as I remember Bill saying in his book: This process develops a decentralizing of "psychic life, which can restrict the strength and functions of the ego. Truth becomes redefined. It is not the province of a single voice, but arises between the voices at the interface of the characters' multiple perspectives" (Watkins, 2000, p. 121). This is extremely important, for it allows a move away from ego psychology's goal of strengthening the ego. "The gradual assimilation of other portions by the ego is no longer the goal" (Watkins, 2000, p. 122). The new goal is to let the figures have voice, let them speak. It is to return some power and voice to the colonies. To this end, one function of personifying is "to save the diversity and autonomy of the psyche from dominion by any single power.... Personifying is the soul's answer to egocentricity" (Hillman, 1975, p. 32).

These views could have been predictable to anyone that knew Bill well. He left the Jung Institute shortly after I was admitted to the training program. I remember him quoting Neruda in one of our last sessions when I sadly and somewhat angrily questioned his leaving. "And something started in my soul, fever or forgotten wings, and I went my own way, deciphering that fire." He smiled and said he had to follow his passion, which was in a different direction than much of modern Jungian theory was heading. He had taken an interest in the body, enactment, imaginations of ways to increase the use of active imagination, and a sense of the importance of story and listening to characters rather than interpreting them. Bill would often quote Miguel Cervantes's words, "Facts are the enemy of truth," when I wanted the definitive theory or explanation to one of my dreams or childhood memories.

The traffic had broken loose during my reveries, and I was finally pulling up to the institute. The parking lot was packed, as expected, but luckily I found a place quickly and snuck in the back door to the auditorium without being noticed. I settled into one of the seats in the last row just as Dr. McIntyre was finishing his talk.

"In closing, I would sum up my greatest yearning and vision for the therapy of psyche," I heard Bill saying as I caught my first glimpse of him at the microphone. Grayer and older, now in his late sixties, but still wearing his favorite shawl-collar sweater and looking much the same as I remembered him from our time together years ago. His voice now raised fervently as he finished his remarks, "It is that of furthering the soul's animation, of allowing her to come to life, speaking and appearing in all varied manners: image, dream, vision, voice, but also hallucinations, body and symptoms, moods and relationships, and lastly, in the world through synchronicities. As Shamdasani says of Jung's *Red Book*, our goal as therapists would be to allow for and promote the lyrical elaboration of psyche's appearance. Bringing her forth more clearly in all the different figures she embodies and distinctly characterizing them to permit their opinions, thoughts, feelings, and wishes to be heard as an equal other in a true I-thou dialogue. This, as we move away from a therapy and a life of 'knowing' interpretations.

"I can hear Hillman's last words, on the last page of his last book, begging to be heard at tonight's ending. 'We are lived by powers we pretend to understand!'" (W. H. Auden, "In Memory of Ernst Toller," 1940, cited in Hillman & Shamdasani, 2013, p. 228).

The applause was strong and indicated to me that his talk had been well received. Bill stood at the podium nodding thank-you as Dr. Peter Huddman, the president of the institute, came to the front and took over the microphone.

"Well, I know we have a lot to discuss after Dr. McIntyre's wonderful and provocative talk, and I am sure it has constellated many reactions and questions in our group," Dr. Huddman said with a look that told me he was having reactions he would like to debate. "He has graciously agreed to take 30 minutes of questions and discussion." As he was speaking, members of the audience had already anticipated his announcement and were moving toward the microphone set up in the middle isle. Dr. Jonas Wolfly, widely considered the dean of analysts in Chicago, was hurriedly leading the way.

Wolfly was a smallish man, of German heritage, nattily dressed in a three-piece tweed suit and carrying a carved walking cane. He was considered by many to be Kohut's greatest interpreter and still commanded immense respect even as he had reached the middle of his ninth decade.

"Dr. McIntyre, it is good to see you after so many years away," Dr. Wolfly started.

"I'm also glad to see you, Dr. Wolfly," Bill replied, preparing himself for what was sure to come.

"What are they doing to you out there on the left coast?" Wolfly smilingly said. "You were such a sensible young man when you took my classes years ago." A clear snicker could be heard through the audience. Bill had done his residency training at the University of Chicago, and Dr. Wolfly had been one of his main supervisors.

Dr. Wolfly continued, "I am not sure why you have turned so severely against the time-tested cudgel of psychoanalysis—interpretation. We at the Chicago school would differ with you significantly on this view, but appreciate your stance on empathy with the other. However, Kohut and modern analysis have already tilled this field by talking about 'experience near' analysis and 'accurate empathy' before proceeding to various levels of interpretation from current dynamic to telescoping genetic when the ground has been properly prepared. You are talking about self and object relationships that get played out in the transference and countertransference, and as Kohut has so clearly shown, become transmuted into new and healthier internalizations through the careful management of the therapeutic relationship and its optimal frustrations. Frankly, Dr. McIntyre, I'm not sure that where you are proposing to take therapy doesn't instead lead us toward the darker ages of our science or at least toward a more superficial and less depthful analysis."

"Well, Dr. Wolfly," Bill began, with a faint smile crossing his face, clearly not offended by anything that had been said. "I have always appreciated your forthrightness, even going back to your thinking I had lost my marbles years ago when I chose to take my analytic training at the Jung Institute instead of the Chicago Institute for Psychoanalysis." Again a slight twitter of laughter could be heard as Dr. Wolfly approvingly nodded his head.

"I appreciate your concerns, and your goal of having a depthful analysis is one I would share," Bill continued. "I stand humbled by the masters of therapy and all they have accomplished and added to our knowledge of the healing arts. You and Dr. Kohut are certainly in that pantheon." Wolfly bowed his head in acknowledgment. "But, and this is crucial, I don't see therapy as only revolving around transference and countertransference relationships, nor do I think interpretation is the main arm of healing the psyche." Bill took a deep breath, a sip of water, and continued.

"Let's take the second point first. I believe the psyche responds to story and longs for story. This is talked about by Jung throughout his collected works. Hillman also spent much of his career reflecting on this issue, using the term *mythopoetic*, meaning the spontaneous story-making tendency of the psyche. I believe that interpretation works when it connects to the story that is accurate for the inner figures. I also believe that 'experience near' interpretations work because they become an external elaboration of an inner figure's thoughts and wishes that as of yet could not be expressed. This can be seen to have huge benefits in treatment. Yet, it can too quickly kill the emerging figure and its still fragile voice, moving toward abstractions, theories, and metapsychological generalizations.

"To your first point, this goes to one of the reasons I went to the Jungian school. When the unconscious is seen as alive and creative in its own right, then the therapeutic relationship is only one way the psyche can be found and worked with. If the figures are as if alive and have voice, then the relationship that may be the most important is the one with them. Remember Jung's famous dictum in his confrontation with the unconscious: 'I...approached them as though they were real people, and listened attentively to what they told me' (Jung, 1973a, p. 181). Let me give an example from one of my cases.

"A woman in her forties had what we might all agree could be called a severe negative mother complex. From a Kohutian view she suffered from a wounded self and formed an idealizing transference. The work brought out a negative, harsh, and punitive mother and a sibling rivalry in classic terms. The mother had set the younger sister up as the ego ideal of attractiveness, family values, and Christian goodness while derogating the patient as carrying all the lesser lights. The patient developed an overwhelming compulsion to steal, particularly pills when she was at work or in a pharmacy, even if she had plenty of her own. She was able to not give in to these urges but was shamed and overwrought with the power of these thoughts. Slowly we were able to gain an 'accurate empathic' sense to her plight and to 'interpret' the dynamics of her negative mother complex and how she had always had to smuggle her needs across her unconscious defenses, lest they never be met. This was all fine and led to improvement in her functioning. She would continue to come in during the working-through phase of treatment and fall back into projecting her mother's cold animus onto me, imaged as an uncaring veterinarian that had come to light in an important dream.

"We continued in this way, using the standard methods common to the field, but one day I realized we were consistently treating all this as an intellectual exercise. The interpretations may have been correct according to different theoretical schools, and we were using the transference relations and helping her to work through breaks in empathy and the slowly occurring optimal frustrations of the idealizing transference, but something was missing. The figures were not alive! They were not approached as if they were real, given voice, and listened to attentively. So one day we more distinctly characterized 'the smuggler.' She was about eight to ten years old and had very painful memories of having all her beautiful hair cut off without anyone caring. I had the patient start to see her and paint her and speak in the session through her thoughts and feelings. She accused the patient of never standing up for her, of giving into the mother and her rigid Christian views. She wanted to dress more provocatively, be more sensual, and be heard when she was in pain and had needs. When we started to let her speak, the course of therapy changed. After years of urges to smuggle pills at work, it was finished. The patient would realize that 'the smuggler' was near. She would talk to her and ask what she needed. She would also stand up to her and have her realize that there were now other ways to get these needs met and that she (the patient self) would help and listen. An I-thou relationship began to occur. Both self and other had a voice and were being heard."

"But Dr. McIntyre, I would have very different viewpoints on what occurred in this case and why it improved," Dr. Wolfly jumped in.

"I am sure, and I can't say you might not be right for your view of the psyche. What we can agree on, however, is that heuristically the patient began to improve substantially when she seemed to be in a real relationship with an as-if other within her own psyche. So if we stay with the phenomenology of what was happening, instead of fighting over Kohutian or classical or Jungian metapsychology, we can see that she began to have a relationship with this imaginal other. When this occurred, she and I had an experience within the therapy of another viewpoint to the story. The therapy involved less of what the 'image or figure means and more of what it wants'" (Hillman, 1983, p. 93).

Dr. Wolfly acknowledged Bill's last reply and then said, "I'm not sure we will ever agree on this subject, but I can see you remember my teachings and are striking out on your own; for that I have the deepest respect." Dr. McIntyre nodded his thanks and the next questioner stepped to the microphone.

I was excited to see it was Dr. Anna Wistram, one of my favorite teachers from my time at the institute. She had received her B.A. in literature from Sarah Lawrence College before going on to obtain her Ph.D. in psychology at Yale. In all the classes she taught at the Jung Institute, she could be counted on to bring amplifications from Shakespeare to Henry Miller, from Virginia Wolf and back to Tolstoy. Her character and carriage displayed a combination of Katherine Hepburn regality and approachable earthiness.

"Anna, it is so good to see you again," Bill said warmly as she approached the microphone.

"Bill, it's a pleasure—both to see you and to experience this wonderful and heartful talk," Anna said in a palpable display of feeling. "I have so long intuited around the edges of what you are more fully explicating tonight. I don't have a specific question as much as a request to possibly elaborate further the idea of characterization you mentioned in your case example with Dr. Wolfly. I am intrigued by this idea; it seems like an expanding of active imagination into actual therapy hours. You also spoke of Robert Olen Butler, the Pulitzer Prize–winning author, as a source of your ideas. I again was selfishly hoping for more about this connection. Also, if I could take just one moment longer, I must quote from memory one of my favorite moments in Gorky's conversations with Tolstoy that I think so wonderfully illustrates your points about the imaginal other."

"That would be a delight, Anna. I know just the story you're about to tell and nothing could exemplify this idea better," Bill answered, clearly pleased that Anna was an ally in this discussion.

"As the story goes, Tolstoy and Gorky were talking, and Gorky remembers the following:

[Tolstoy] rubbed his chest hard over the heart, raised his eyebrows, and then, remembering something, went on: "One autumn in Moscow in an alley near the Sukhariot Gate I once saw a drunken woman lying in the gutter. A stream of filthy water flowed from the yard of a house right under her neck and back. She lay in that cold liquid, muttering, shivering, wriggling her body in the wet, but she could not get up."

He shuddered, half closed his eyes, shook his head, and went on gently: "Let's sit down here... It's the most horrible and disgusting thing, a drunken woman. I wanted to help her get up, but I couldn't; I felt such a loathing; she was so slippery and slimy I felt that if I'd touched her, I could not have washed my hand clean for a month—horrible! And on the curb sat a bright, gray-eyed boy, the tears running down his cheeks: he was sobbing and repeating wearily and helplessly: 'Muum...mu-um-my....do get up.' She would move her arms, grunt, lift her head, and again—back went her neck into the filth."

He was silent, and then looking round, he repeated almost in a whisper: "Yes, yes, horrible! You've seen many drunken women? Many—my God! You, you must not write about that, you mustn't."

"Why?"

He looked straight into my eyes and smiling repeated: "Why?" Then thoughtfully and slowly he said: "I don't know. It just slipped out ...it's a shame to write about filth. But yet why not write about it? Yes, it's necessary to write all about everything, everything."Tears came into his eyes. He wiped them away and smiling, he looked at his handkerchief, while the tears again ran down his wrinkles. "I am crying," he said. "I am an old man. It cuts me to the heart when I remember something horrible."

And very gently touching me with his elbow, he said, "You, too—you will have lived your life, and everything will remain exactly as it was, and then you, too, will cry worse than I, more 'streamingly,' as the peasant women say. And everything must be written about, everything; otherwise that bright little boy might be hurt, he might reproach us —'it's untrue, it's not the whole truth,' he will say. He's strict for the truth" (Gorky, 1920, pp. 80–82).

The emotional silence penetrated the lecture hall. Anna quietly returned to her seat, a tear noticeable on her cheek. Bill stood at the lectern for what seemed like minutes before speaking. "I can't thank Dr. Wistram enough for sharing that extraordinary story with us. Everything that I have wanted to say tonight is encapsulated in that example. If I may, I will use this story to address some of Anna's requests." The audience, still mesmerized by the tale's emotional power, silently assented.

"There is so much that can be said regarding this," Bill began. "Let's start with what happened, in my view, with Tolstoy. He 'suddenly sees through the gray eyes of that "bright little boy" and reverses his stance. At first he had automatically sought Gorky's promise to ignore the drunken woman.' But through his tears 'he becomes aware of the price of ignorance'—the exclusion of the little boy. This allows the voice and figure of the boy to begin to confront Tolstoy. 'It's untrue, it's not the whole truth' (Watkins, 2000, p. 156). This shift is the key to what I am championing tonight. It is the shift to the viewpoint of the little boy by Tolstoy. It is this 'that distinguishes a psychotherapy which respects the autonomy and necessity of imaginal figures. In such a therapy one turns outside of the...habitual ego responses to the characters in order to hear from them...their truths. The ego stance changes from ignoring to observing'" (Watkins, 2000, p. 156).

Bill looked at his audience to see their responses. These ideas were the heart of his premise, and he wanted to drive them home.

"This is the same idea I was suggesting in my example with Dr. Wolfly," Bill continued. "There was no deep change in character until the voice of 'the smuggler' was heard and appreciated as other, until the patient herself could see through the other's eyes and hear her voice. When it is fully grasped and appreciated that it seems as if the psyche is inherently dialogical and dramatic in its presentations, then the job of the analyst changes. It becomes one of helping 'make explicit the various voices [and figures] it contains' (Watkins, 2000, p. 156).

"Now this is very exciting," Bill said as he was clearly stimulated by the direction the discussion was now heading. "Dr. Wistram mentioned her intuition that much of what I have been saying leads toward an expansion of active imagination. I would completely agree. Remember in my closing remarks I mentioned *The Red Book* and lyrical elaboration. As a therapist I'm looking for all the channels and ways the characters that are outside of the ego may emerge, and I am also treating the ego as a character itself, sometimes momentary and sometimes habitual. But, and this is crucial, he or she is just one character in the story.

"For instance, if a person comes in with depression and anxiety and as she talks about the experience of it, she shows me how her legs and arms are twitching and jumping during the day and how they feel an overwhelming sense of heaviness, then I want to go further with this sensory-grounded description. This is where Dr. Wistram's referral to Robert Olen Butler becomes useful. Olen Butler has written a superb book on writing titled *From Where You Dream*. In it he has wonderful insights that I feel apply as much to therapy as they do writing fiction. This would take us too far afield tonight to discuss the idea of therapy as fiction instead of science, but as I'm sure many of you know, Havelock Ellis thought Freud was writing as an artist, and Hillman wrote a wonderful article along this line called 'The Fiction of Case History.'

"I was originally drawn to Olen Butler when I read these core premises in his book's introduction, by Janet Burroway, and put analyst or therapist in place of writer: 1. The imagination of the writer [therapist] 'must be a strong and supple instrument, ready to lead the reader [patient] through moment-by-moment sensual experience.' 2. '[I]t is in the realm of the unconscious rather than that of technique or intellect that the writer [analyst] seeks fictional truth.' 3. 'The primary point of contact for the reader [patient] is...an emotional one, because emotions reside in the senses' and therefore generalizations, analysis, and abstraction lead us away from these emotional experiences (Olen Butler, 2005, p. 2), and in our case, away from the individual experience of the figures. All imaginal figures become known through the elaboration and amplification of the senses.

"Let's go back to the example of the woman with the anxious depression and the somatic experience of heaviness, muscle jerks, and twitching," Bill continued. "The heaviness indicates two figures already present. One is experiencing the heavy feeling masquerading as the abstraction called depression. This is the figure closest to the patient ego or current 'self' figure, but not fully characterized and in an amalgam with the 'other' at this juncture. The second figure is the one making the heaviness. There are various ways to intervene here. One could work proprioceptively and bring out more distinctly these two figures, but I chose to work in the kinesthetic or movement channel because of the jumping muscle symptoms in her arms and legs.

"I asked her to stand and begin to walk back and forth across my office in a normal manner, while noticing what part of herself was not wanting to walk or seemed incongruent to her normal way of walking. Though she was a new patient, she took to this method of therapy quickly and enthusiastically, and noticed her right leg wanting to drag behind her slightly. As we increased and amplified this signal, a figure began to emerge. The patient became like a woman wounded and weighted down, dragging her leg behind her and bent over in her upper body, as if she were pulling heroically against a behemoth that was almost winning the battle. Tears and moaning arose and words came painfully, saying, 'This is too hard, I can't make it.' I pointed out to her that she seemed to be pulling against a huge other power, and the patient said it felt like she was caught in brambles or tar and was trying with all her might to break free. Now we began to draw out this tar-brambles energy as I became the patient fighting against it, and the patient became the bramble force herself.

"I said, 'No, I will never give up. I am going to break free!'

"The patient suddenly exclaimed with the voice of this other power, 'Never! You should be ashamed to have thoughts like that about your marriage; that is not Christian. I will never let you free!' She was shocked that this had come out of her mouth, and we were now more fully aware of the figures that were emerging, and seeing more clearly the source of the unconscious conflict. We began to connect this to her everyday life and to an understanding of the story of her depression and symptoms as they began to unfold.

"You can see in this example, as in the others discussed, the beginnings of characters emerging through different so-called channels. In the smuggler example the other was slowly brought to light in the story of the therapy, and then a conscious transit was made to see through her perspective. In the Gorky example Tolstoy remembers the little boy in the telling of his old memory and then feels him when the tears emerge. A spontaneous transit to the other takes place. In the current example the patient was able to experience the absolute archetypal and witchlike spell that had been cast over her when she embodied the figures from within the movement channel, and then the heaviness of her depressive symptoms could be understood as the hint from her psyche of the battle that was being waged in her unconscious for her very existence.

"The key now is to characterize these emerging figures more fully, not to quickly retreat to various theories of mothers, fathers, ids, superegos, shadows, or archetypes. The figures are not being made; they are being discovered. Elizabeth Bowen has a wonderful saying, 'One cannot make characters, only marionettes' (Bowen, 1975, p. 172). Our job now becomes the lyrical elaboration of these characters. We must enhance their animation, further the articulation of psychological properties, increase the complexity of perspective, and make more distinct the specification of their identity (Watkins, 2000, pp. 118–119). All this can occur through encouraging enacting, art, writing, conversation, and many other forms of deepening the involvement with them. As in comments from great novelists who talk about living with their characters and getting to know the moment to moment of what they might think or eat, you are asking your patients to begin to live more consciously with their imaginal others and know them more intimately. Now in my opinion the therapy I am imagining moves closer to art. The goal becomes 'artistic truth, and not literal truth'" (Olen Butler, 2001).

Bill glanced at his watch. The 30 minutes of questions had now become over an hour.

"I just looked at the time and realized it's getting late. I apologize for not getting to more questions, but those last thoughts really captured my imagination," Bill said as Dr. Huddman approached the lectern, agreeing that we should call it a night.

"I would like to say thanks to all of you for coming and again to Dr. McIntyre for an inspiring question and discussion portion of his talk to end our night. I know there are many more thoughts to be examined and reflected on. I, for one, would love to have Bill back soon to continue exploring all that was brought up." The applause made it obvious that most agreed. Now the usual procession to the front began, similar to needing to shake the minister's hand when leaving the church. I waited patiently, as I wanted to spend a minute with Bill to reconnect. I had hoped to have breakfast with him in the morning, but when we emailed he said he was going back on the red-eye the same night. There was an important project he was negotiating, and he would tell me more later. Finally the line cleared, and I headed to the front.

A big smile from both of us and a warm hug marked a far-too-long-awaited reconnection in person. The obligatory back and forth of "you're looking good" followed, but before much more could be said, Bill realized he had to leave immediately or take the chance of missing his flight. He grabbed my hand and looked me straight in the eyes.

"I'm going back to negotiate a deal for a building where I'll be opening a clinic and possibly a school to teach therapy in the way I talked about tonight. We are looking for some psychiatry and analytic types," he said with a smile. "Love to have you on the left coast." He jumped into Peter Huddman's car to head for the airport before I could quite digest what he was suggesting. As they pulled out into the Chicago night, he put his hand up to his ear in the universal sign language for phone and mouthed, "Call me."

The drive home was full of memories of the talk and wonderful ideas to reflect upon. But most of my thoughts went to his last-minute clinic revelation. My wife and I had always lived in Chicago. We were homegrown. Both of our kids had moved out to Oregon and California, but I had not wanted to follow. I had my dream job at a powerful university. I would be tenured in another three years and set for life. I would be eligible to be a training analyst at the Jung Institute within the next year. But I also remembered today's drive to the institute and the sense that maybe my wife had been right years ago. Rumi's words, translated by Andrew Harvey, came echoing into my ear, "Futile solutions deceive the force of passion. They are banded to extort money through lies. Marshy and stagnant water is no cure for thirst. No matter how limpid and delicious it might look, it will only stop and prevent you from looking for fresh rivers...."

I pulled into the driveway and got out of the car with a new bounce in my step. Opening the door I saw my wife sitting and reading. She had waited up to hear about the lecture. Before she could say anything, I said, "You know how you have been wanting to be closer to the kids on the West Coast?"

ANIMAL EYES

THE MARIMBA RING tones tugged relentlessly at my sleep. Chicago is two hours later than the West Coast, and my friend and former analyst Dr. William McIntyre clearly had miscalculated the timing of his call.

"Tom," I heard Bill say with a pressured feel to his greeting. I grabbed my glasses at the bedside and shot a look at the clock.

"Bill, what's up? Is everything okay?" I replied, slowly coming to consciousness as my wife pulled the pillow over her head in hopes of falling back to sleep.

"Do you remember my telling you about the idea for a clinic when I was hurrying to catch the red-eye home last week?"

"Of course I do," I quickly replied. "Elaine and I are still seriously talking about your offer and very much considering a move. Sorry I didn't get back to you."

"No, no, I wasn't upset about not hearing from you, but I do need you now!" Bill said quite forcefully. "This is one hell of a story I have to tell you." But before I had a chance to say "let's talk tomorrow," Bill was already telling his tale.

"The main donor for the clinic is Kirima Holder, an amazing woman from the Inupiat culture in Alaska. Her great-grandfather was a well-respected shaman and seer in their village. However, despite this prominent standing in her community, she became disgruntled with her life during her adolescence and rebelled against her tribal roots, marrying a wealthy oilman and quickly having three children. Their marriage was a rocky one and stints of couples counseling were all that kept it patched together. But as the children grew she realized she wanted them to have a connection to their aboriginal heritage and its myths and stories. Her husband absolutely forbade this, always asserting that this was a primitive way of life, and he didn't want his children brought up with anything but a good Catholic foundation and Jesus Christ as their savior.

"Mr. Holder was tragically stricken with lung cancer one year ago and died just six weeks short of his diagnostic date. Before dying, however, his Saturnian power made one last attempt to affect his children's fate. He expected them to follow in his footsteps, finishing college in business and raising their families as devout Christians. Kirima said that these demands were fine for her youngest two. They had very much followed her husband's more modern ways and seemed naturally suited for this style of life. She, however, had worried about her oldest. Alignak, as her great-grandfather had called him, meant "god of the moon." His Christian name was Alex, but he had always preferred Alignak, much to the chagrin of his father. He was a dreamer and his interests included nature, poetry, literature, and the history of his race. When he went off to college last year, his father threatened to cut off tuition when Alex declared his plan to major in ancient religions. But these threats did not deter him, because he had always bravely followed his own way. He unflinchingly stood for his beliefs, even in the face of his father's constant shaming and name calling. Their relationship, when together, devolved into ever-increasing shouting matches. By the time hospice was called for terminal care, both had refused to be in each other's presence, and in the end Alignak even refused his mother's pleading and chose not to attend the funeral.

"But something changed in his behavior shortly after his father's death. He became increasingly withdrawn. He stopped getting up to run in the morning, and stayed up late into the night, often sitting silently, staring into the fire, with Mircea Eliade's book *Shamanism: Archaic Techniques of Ecstasy* always by his side. He dropped out of school, spoke less and less, and conversed only if he was directly addressed. Kirima said that if any of the family questioned him, he would often stare with the most penetrating, piercing gaze, his eyes narrowing as if he were looking into their soul. Then one evening when out with friends, she received a frantic phone call from his brothers. Alignak was perched on the refrigerator, with all the lights out, crouched as if an animal hunting prey. He was taken to the hospital and placed in their locked psychiatric ward."

"Whew, what a powerful story!" I responded, fascinated as always by the imaginations and behaviors of this alternate reality psychiatry calls psychosis. "However, I still don't understand what prompted the call tonight."

"Kirima is begging me to treat her son, and I can't. I am starting on a book tour next week and will be traveling throughout the United States and Europe for over a month," Bill said, becoming clearer about his wishes. "Anyway, this is your area of expertise. You were friends with John Perry and used to treat first-break psychosis without medications in your residency."

"I haven't done that type of work in 25 years, except for a smattering of cases, and they had all been on medications," I quickly responded, a little stunned at what he was suggesting. "And what do medications have to do with this? Is he not taking any?"

"He is refusing antipsychotics, and his mother is backing him. She believes something important is happening that might have to do with her great-grandfather and their shamanistic background. The hospital doctors are very upset with her and want to have the courts force the issue. It is quite the scene."

I could feel both my excitement and apprehension rising. Bill knew that he could make my automatic "no" waver just by mentioning John Perry and my residency days. Working with psychotic patients had been my passion when I first started training. I had met John in medical school during a psychiatric rotation in San Francisco. Dr. Perry had just reopened Diabasis House and was treating first-break psychosis in an unlocked facility in the city. This treatment is well documented in papers describing the Agnews Project designed by him and Julian Silverman. They established the first inpatient hospital treatment funded by grants from NIMH to document research treating acute psychosis off medications. Perry also further documented this approach in his books *The Self in Psychotic Process* and *The Far Side of Madness*.

The medical model of psychosis and schizophrenia states that this is a biomedical illness and requires medications. If there is a psychological component, which is seen as doubtful, it is imagined in the regressive light of early family dynamics and a weak ego structure. In his work at Burgholzli documented in *The Psychology of Dementia Praecox*, Jung (2015) had shown that there was meaning hidden in these bizarre thoughts and behaviors. He postulated that this breakdown, at least in some instances, was an extreme version of a natural process brought on by the psyche to renew itself—a sense of going back to the matrix to come forward again in a healthier manner. "Weller than well," as Karl Menninger was to call some of the treatment responses of his schizophrenic patients. Dr. Perry had followed this belief, expounding on it with historical parallels to visionaries and how the experiences of their individual psychology mirrored the larger culture's need for radical change in times of crisis. At about this same time in San Jose, these findings were duplicated by Loren Mosher's Soteria House project and earlier in London with R. D. Laing's work at Kingsley Hall.

I devoured these works by Perry, Mosher, Laing, and Jung and modeled their approach in the fourth year of my residency by attempting to treat first-break psychotic patients on an inpatient ward with psychotherapy but without medications. But the times and the prevailing theories of psychosis had now hardened into a biological monopoly. Even though it has been shown that there was at least a small cohort of patients who had an excellent prognosis after having their first psychotic episode and without being given neuroleptic medications (Carpenter, 1977, pp. 14–20), current teachings and treatment make no room for this way of imagining. Pursuing Perry's treatment course today opens one up to ridicule at best and malpractice at worst. And, of course, I would have to suddenly drop my responsibilities at the University of Chicago. Dr. Riback, my department chair, would take a dim view of my leaving.

"In your hesitancy to answer I can hear your consideration of my plea, but also concern over all the responsibilities at your practice that would make it impossible to leave," Bill said, reading my thoughts. "Well, I anticipated this. I have spoken to Dr. Riback. He and I were classmates during our residency at the University of Chicago, and we have remained close friends. He has agreed to a four-week sabbatical, along with full pay, the only caveat being that you give grand rounds upon returning and publish an article on the case."

"I'm surprised—why is he being so generous and accommodating?" I asked, knowing that Dr. Riback was not prone to offer paid sabbaticals.

"He is very interested in the literature coming out of the National Institute of Mental Health's RAISE program research on schizophrenia treatment and the compelling reports that have emanated from Finland through the years and their amazing success compared to the standard approaches taken in the United States. He is hoping that your Jungian viewpoint would dovetail with the work coming out of the Chicago Medical School on self psychological perspectives in treating psychosis by David Garfield and Ira Steinman. His vision is to create a more psychologically oriented approach to this population's treatment in Chicago and at the university, where the depth psychological perspective can reclaim its rightful place in training and treatment that the hegemony of the biological position has currently usurped.

"Please know also that housing is taken care of. Connie and I will be traveling the next month, and we have plenty of room for you and Elaine. Since you were thinking of moving anyway, the two of you could consider this a 'how do we like the West Coast' trip. Anyway,

Elaine has been trying to get you to move out here for years to be closer to your grandchild, and Seattle is a lot closer than Chicago."

The clock at our bedside nightstand now read one o'clock, and I had to be up for work in five hours. I needed to talk with my wife before any decision could be made. I also needed some sleep.

"I'll call you tomorrow after speaking with Elaine. If I decide to do this, how soon do you need me?"

"Yesterday," Bill said with a laugh playing through his voice.

I put the phone down and cozied up next to my sleeping wife. Talking tomorrow would be soon enough; shutting off my racing thoughts and getting some rest was all that was immediately important.

Just three days later we were settling into our first-class seats on the red-eye out of Chicago O'Hare headed for Seattle. Tickets had been hard to find, and we owed our fancy accommodations to Kirima since she was willing to do anything to bring us west straightaway. Elaine was quite excited about the adventure and looking forward to seeing more of the West Coast. Our son lived in Los Angeles, and our daughter, son-in-law, and grandson in Bend, Oregon. They had been after us for years to think about moving, but I was always adamant that I couldn't leave my dream job at the university. Now my wife spied a crack in the armor and was more than ready to exploit it. It was 8:00 p.m. and we were about to endure eight hours of travel, arriving finally in Seattle at 2:00 a.m.

I nestled into the soft leather chair and accepted my free glass of Pinot. I was hoping the wine would help me relax and get some rest as I had promised Bill and Ms. Holder I would be at the Harborview Medical Center by 9 a.m. I sipped my drink and shut my eyes while images of past patients flooded my memories. Coincident with the images was the same gut-level feeling that had plagued me for years. At my core I had always known that the current doctrinaire theory informing my profession—treating all psychotic patients in locked wards with short stays, pathological pronouncements, and high-dose medications—was wrong. But almost as quickly as that view entered my awareness, I could hear the rumbling rebuttal of my inner biological shrink making his counterattack.

"Are you saying there is no place for medications, diagnosis, or locked units in the treatment of psychosis?" came the quick retort. This was the way these arguments always went, either-or, one way or the other. No room for subtlety and nuance. I agree with this inner arbiter of psychiatric dogma some of the time. I had experienced how medications can perform miracles on hopeless cases. I remember a father pleading with me to help his son who was not eating and was carving tattoos into his chest, thinking he was evil incarnate. He was treated with Clozaril in a locked state hospital facility and recovered so completely that he was now working with his father on the family farm. I had also witnessed the tragedy of patients haunted by voices, trapped in their delusions, taking their own lives, and in rare instances the lives of others. These stories of treatment success cannot be underestimated.

"But, and this is a crucial but," I responded to my theoretical antagonist. "I believe that psychiatrists and psychiatric training have lost the middle way, and this shows itself most profoundly in the treatment of psychosis. By treating all patients with psychotic presentations as if solely biological in their cause, psychiatric theory literalizes delusions and hallucinations into the physis of brain chemistry. This automatically leads to the imagination of exclusively physical treatments. In the past this included bleeding, dunking, spinning, lobotomies, metrazol seizure inducements, and insulin coma, reprehensibly interspersed for a period of time with sterilization brought on by a eugenics mentality, only to be replaced today with electroshock and polypharmacy" (Whitaker, 2002).

In this way of conceptualizing, the middle ground of imagination and the symbolic, metaphor and the as-if, has no place in modern psychiatric education. To work with psychotic patients the *metaxy* or in-between is key because it is through this reality of dreaming that

they live and see the world. Without training and access to the phe-
nomenological underpinnings of this "separate reality," psychiatrists
are left instead with their only guides becoming the plethora of overintellectualized textbooks filled with the metapsychological grids of
theories and explanations. A recent patient's story shows this point
quite well.

Melody, a woman in her late forties when her first psychotic episode occurred, was hospitalized after she became paranoid, believing
there was a man in her yard threatening to break into her home. She
was admitted to the psychiatric unit against her will and placed on a
72-hour hold. She cleared without medications and was released after
a work-up found no organic etiology. Melody came to see me in my
office, and as we talked for the first time, she told me of the very real
fear of having had planes spy on her and of the intruder that seemed
so alive in her experience.

As I recalled this first meeting, I took another sip of my wine and
remembered her plaintive response.

"How can all of you psychiatrists be so sure there were no planes
spying on me and no men lurking in my backyard?" she asked, her
question sounding much more like a condemnation of her recent treatment. "It seemed so real to me and still does. But I was told by every
nurse and doctor at the hospital that this is all a delusion, an illness, a
trick of my mind; that it had no meaning in my life; that I should move
on and chalk it up to faulty wiring and poor chemical communication." She stopped and took a deep breath, looked down at the floor,
then slowly raised her gaze toward mine, a hint of a tear running down
her cheek. "Doc, it seemed so real!"

I sat quietly with my eyes closed, allowing myself to feel the full
weight and pain of her question before responding. "Melody, I agree
with you. There is no way that I or any other person can say your encounter was not real," I gently replied.

"So, are you saying the planes were real and so was the intruder?"
she asked, clearly surprised by my response.

"I can't say it wasn't, only that other people were not seeing or having your same experience. What I can say, without hesitation, is that these events were real to you and to see them as random 'faulty wiring' is not a story that allows you to make meaningful sense of them. But what if it doesn't have to be either way, that the psychiatrists are literally right or you are literally right. What if there is a middle ground, a reality that's just as real as the outer, literal world because it is happening to you. I can't say there was or wasn't a man in your yard last week, but I *can* say there is an intruder trying to break into your inner psychic house, no different from bringing me a dream with the same motif. If you came to a session and told me, "Doctor, I had a dream last night that a man was trying to break into my home, then I woke up and thought, 'Oh, that was just a dream,' I would tell you, 'No, it is really happening psychologically, you must take it seriously, as if it were real.'"

"Wow, that's heavy. So you are saying it is all in my mind, but it is just as real there?" she asked, open to but confused about this new way of thinking.

"Yes, that's exactly right. Again, I can't say it didn't happen out in the world, but I can say it happened in your inner world. I can also say that your dreaming world got so strong because it wasn't being paid enough attention, and then the world became your dream. To the outer world that will look 'crazy,' but it is just you 'dreaming while awake.'"

At this point in my reminiscences my own Doubting Thomas of psychological reality decided to fire off one more salvo, "This is an intervention that can work when a patient's ego observer is still intact. It really is not much different from Freud's position in the Schreber case. This is not the typical situation with psychotic patients, who tend to present completely engulfed by the unconscious. You cannot have this type of conversation or therapy with them; medication becomes the only humane intervention."

The last comment had affected me. I knew only too well that I had not worked with acutely psychotic patients in this way for many years. Would I be able to do therapy with a young man who sat on kitchen appliances thinking he was a predatory animal? I was not sure, and my inner critic knew this. My concern and uncertainty kept me awake.

The captain's voice announced preparation for landing in Phoenix. As we pulled our "seatbacks and tray tables to their full upright positions," complying with the standard landing instructions of our flight attendant, Elaine touched my hand softly and said, "You look exhausted, Tom. I can tell you're worrying over this case. Please get some sleep on this next leg, or you won't be any good to him in the morning." I smiled at her, nodding my okay as I leaned over and gave her a soft kiss on the cheek. She knew me so well after our many years together.

The "prepare for takeoff" command from the flight deck couldn't have come soon enough. We had been delayed two hours in Phoenix because of engine trouble and were now due to arrive in Seattle at 4:00 a.m. West Coast time. I was, as Elaine had noted, dog-tired, and instead of the glass of wine offered by the attendant I asked for a pillow and blanket. After we attained our cruising altitude, I lay back for a much needed siesta.

I grabbed the cold, gray metal railing to head up the stairs from the ground floor entrance of my high school. The entrance was in the back corner of the building with two doors leading outside into the open fields. As I was about to begin my climb to the classrooms, I realized I was not alone. Pacing the concrete foyer just a few feet away was a large black panther, his movements deft, his body supple, his carriage graceful, but his piercing eyes by far his most arresting feature. His stare penetrated me, and I was like a deer caught frozen in headlights on a country road. He moved toward the railing, not in a threatening way, but still my fear was unmistakable as my lips dried, heart pounded, and hands quivered. Suddenly, a sound began repeating from the dark corner underneath the stairwell, and the panther responded as if to his master. "SLOOOOOOW, SLOOOOOOOW, SLOOOOOOW" came the words of a voice struggling to speak. A small man emerged from the shadows, crumpled in body, his right leg dragging from an obvious paralysis, his right arm crippled, his right facies contorted. The panther now moved toward him as he looked with his one good eye first at the panther, then upward at me. He continued to mouth painfully the word SLOOOOOOOW, with the panther now rubbing against him like a common house cat. He began to pet this amazing animal across the head and back in the most loving manner, all the while continuing his mantra, SLOOOOOOW. Then he turned toward me and, reaching out with his one working arm, seemed to be begging me to pet the panther...SLOWLY.

Elaine nudged me awake. "Tom, you were dreaming and talking in your sleep," she said with an enjoying chuckle.

"What was I saying?" I asked, slightly embarrassed at the thought that others may have heard me.

"It was garbled, but it sounded like the word *slow.*"

"I remember now," I said excitedly. "There was a crippled man in my dream. He was the Quasimodo-like figure that came to me when I was doing the active imagination with Jung a few weeks back. He was petting a black panther and imploring me to do the same while he said the word *slow.* The panther was a stunning creature with the most startling, intense eyes."

Before I could say anything further about the dream, Elaine interrupted. "Didn't you tell me that Kirima had described her son as having a piercing stare during the beginning of his psychosis? Could there be a possible connection?"

"That's a great intuition, honey," I replied, my mind beginning to race with possibilities. The dream seemed to say the animal had to be approached slowly, carefully, but that he was now the teacher, not the standard classroom teachers above. Intellectual book learning would have to be put aside, it was the ground floor of the body and instincts that would now instruct. And what about the same piercing gaze? Were Alignak's and my fate intertwined? It definitely felt like the dream was somehow connected with my upcoming work with him.

The plane began its descent for landing in Seattle. I was looking forward to meeting this young man who already was affecting my unconscious.

Harborview Medical Center is the main teaching hospital for the University of Washington Medical School and cuts an impressive picture as part of the Seattle skyline. Built originally in 1877 as the six-bed King County Hospital, it moved locations and took its present form in 1931. The Medical Center is now a 413-bed facility with 61 of those dedicated to their psychiatric inpatient units. It is owned by King County and treats the majority of indigent patients and involuntary admissions for the area.

Entering the west wing of the medical complex off 8th Street, I headed down the hallway to the beautiful courtyard art display, where we had agreed to meet. Arriving after a few minutes' walk, I could see Bill sitting across the plaza with an attractive woman of native descent. They sat talking, each with the ubiquitous Starbucks double grande in hand and what was apparently one for me sitting on the table between them. He waved happily as he saw me approaching.

"Tom, it's great to see you," Bill said, standing to shake my hand. "This is Kirima Holder. I have been telling her about your work."

"Dr. Harper, I can't thank you enough for coming to help my son," Ms. Holder enthused, seemingly rising to take my extended hand but instead suddenly placing me in an appreciative embrace. She was a woman in her late thirties, petite, with shoulder-length, raven-black hair, high cheek bones, and deep-set brown eyes accentuating the warmth of her smile.

"My pleasure, Ms. Holder. I am looking forward to working with Alignak. I'm also hoping Dr. McIntyre didn't overstate my abilities." Everyone laughed as Bill feigned personal injury from my remark. We then spent time covering the usual amenities of conversation: how was the flight, how are the kids, where was Elaine, Bill and Connie's upcoming trip to Europe, and then most important, how was Alignak?

"He just sits and stares," Ms. Holder said, taking a long, slow breath attempting to calm the panic of a mother's pain. "He is eating and drinking very little and has lost at least 15 pounds since this has all started. Dr. Stegmeyer, the head of psychiatry, has been quite kind, but he has also made it clear that they are going to take Alignak to court in another seven days, based on grave disability, unless he begins to care for himself."

"Have they given him any medications yet?" I asked.

"No, Dr. Stegmeyer understands my wishes, and Alignak has refused any offerings."

"So, he just sits all day by himself, not talking or interacting with anyone?"

"He sits, sometimes up on one of the tables in the corner, seeming to prefer height, and there he stares out, for hours, eyes squinting, looking around, hypervigilant and paranoid perhaps, but more like an animal acutely aware of all that is happening in his surroundings. He hasn't spoken, even to me, since being taken to the hospital," Kirima said, her voice dropping once more into her deep sadness.

"Bill, didn't you tell me that when this first happened Alignak was perched on top of the refrigerator, and that his brothers said he looked like an animal stalking his prey?" I asked.

Bill quickly nodded, saying, "Yes, what are you getting at? Do you think the animal is important?" Before I could answer, Kirima jumped in.

"My great-grandfather's spirit animal was the wolf, and the name given to him after he became a shaman was 'Isumatturuk Amaguk' in our native language, or 'Wise Wolf' in English."

"Tell us about your great-grandfather, if you would," Bill said.

"He was a wonderful man, and we were quite close. Great Father, as I called him, was quite devastated when I fought with my mother and left the community at sixteen. My father died when I was five, and my grandfather before I was born, so my great-grandfather and my mother raised me. He was always quite mystical, at times staring at you with his unblinking gaze and then saying something that was often quite shocking in its effect on your life. I remember sitting with him in the morning when members of our village would come to tell him their dreams from the night before—one of his shamanic duties. He would sit silently, sometimes taking the hand of the dreamer in his, and then stare, trancelike, his eyes squinting as if he were looking straight through them to some distant world. A shake of his head would soon follow, and he would be back in the present, happy or sad, depending on what he had seen in his vision. With the greatest compassion he would then share his information from the other realm, interpreting how to incorporate the dreaming world's message into everyday life."

Kirima stopped speaking for just a moment, clearly moved by these memories as she reached to wipe a tear from her eye. "I think about him often and miss him always," she said quietly.

"An amazing man, Kirima," I said. "I would have loved to have spent time with him, as I am sure he could have taught academic shrinks like myself a thing or two about the living unconscious."

Bill nodded his head and said, "I couldn't agree more."

"Thank you both," Kirima said. "I'm sure you're right about his having something to teach, especially with psychiatry's focus on treating symptoms only with drugs. Great Father was called to his profession by dreams and symptoms and through his initiation rites by mentoring shamans. His knowledge came from direct experience by connecting to his spirit helpers. This connection to what you just called 'the living unconscious,' or what my great father would have called the *irrusik,* or inner man, seems to have been lost in most of our current academic programs and psychological schools, and it's why I am calling on you to help with Alignak and giving Bill money for a new clinic. I can see in Bill's work and what he has told me of you, Tom, that the spirit of my great-grandfather would have been brother to Jung's and is still alive in both of you."

"Powerfully said," Bill replied, and I silently nodded my head. "I hope Tom and I can live up to your vision for a different and more experiential healing for patients in all states of consciousness."

"I'd like to add one more piece to the story and explain why I am so convinced that this is also a calling for Alignak as it was for Great Father," Kirima continued. "He was born just as my great father became sick and wasn't long for this existence. He asked to spend as much time with Alignak as possible. He told me they could teach each other about their worlds. My great-grandfather knew about the world Alignak was entering and he was leaving, and my son could teach him about the one he had just left and that my great father was soon to enter.

"I had to sneak off with Alignak to see him, since my husband was quite angry with me and disliked my great-grandfather. Great Father began calling him Alignak instead of Alex, based on the visions he was having when he would hold and rock him, seeing the moon, full and lighting up the night sky. Shortly before he died, while holding Alignak for the last time, he said to me, 'He is special, Kirima; called, as was I. I can see it in him. Know that someday he will bay at the moon; don't be frightened when this happens. Get him to a healer and all will be well.'

"That's why I have called you both," Kirima added. "My hope is that we can reach him and get him back to my people, who will know what to do and the healing he needs." Suddenly, as if remembering something important, she glanced at her watch, clearly surprised at the time. "Nine forty-five, I hadn't realized we talked so long. I promised Dr. Stegmeyer that we would meet him at his office by ten o'clock sharp. It's a little bit of a hike across campus, so we should get started."

We rose together and I looked over at Bill to ask if he was coming. "I'm going to let you handle this alone," Bill replied. "I have a few last-minute things to do before Connie and I head out tomorrow. I'll see you back at the house tonight and the four of us can go out for dinner and catch up.

"Listen, Paul Stegmeyer is a great guy, well versed in all the latest studies on schizophrenia, including the psychotherapeutic. You'll like him. He is a throwback to the renaissance men and women who used to be called to our profession." We gave each other a hug, and I followed Kirima back across the plaza, knowing this meeting with Dr. Stegmeyer was crucial in establishing any chance of the successful treatment of her son.

⮾

Paul Stegmeyer, M.D., sat in his office, staring thoughtfully out the window as he looked across the Seattle skyline. Nothing like what was about to transpire had ever happened in his 30-plus years of practicing psychiatry, 15 of them as chief of the inpatient psychiatric units for the University of Washington Medical School. He was a full professor of psychiatry, for God's sake, well-known in academic circles for his research and expertise in schizophrenia, called to lecture across the country on various topics, author of multiple articles for major medical journals and a book on inpatient treatment methods using a biopsychosocial model, and yet he was allowing an oil-rich widow to bring in a Jungian analyst from Chicago, whom he had never heard of, to consult on her son and his patient.

Technically, Alex was not his patient; he knew that. Richard Ruthafurd was the head psychiatrist of Ward 5-West, and he and a fourth-year psychiatric resident were the physicians of record on this case. He often felt, though, like a protective father since taking the job as chief years ago, and that all patients admitted to the psychiatric wards were ultimately his responsibility. To that end, he rounded daily to keep a close eye on his flock. In this case, however, he was called in by Dr. Ruthafurd because of its high-profile nature, as Kirima Holder was a large donor to the university, and also because the presentation of Alex was so unusual.

Since being admitted by a DMHP, designated mental health professional, about 10 days earlier on a 72-hour involuntary hold, Alex had rarely moved from his roosting spot on a table in the corner of the community room. He sat on his haunches for hours, his eyes constantly moving, like an animal wary of danger. The night staff said he often remained like this through the shift, though he would occasionally sleep for short periods. They had been able to place a blanket over him at those times, but if they approached him with food or tried to get him down from the table so they could take him to his assigned room, he would bare his teeth and growl. He had not taken any food since his admission, but was still drinking water. He would occasionally climb down to go to his room to relieve himself, but just as quickly come back to his perch on the table, not yet saying a word to anyone since his entry to the unit.

The doctors had elected to hold him for a later court hearing based on grave disability, alleging that he couldn't care for his needs if released. The court agreed to a 14-day hold before the hearing, and now just seven days were left. However, Ms. Holder had obtained private legal counsel for Alex, and they were asking for a jury trial. It had created quite the uproar on the ward, with various staff taking sides for or against forced treatment, and Dr. Ruthafurd taking a very vocal position about the stupidity of anyone and everyone who questioned the scientific rationale of modern medication treatment for this well-proven and obviously biological disease. This had led to some intense discussions between Dr. Stegmeyer and Dr. Ruthafurd. Ruthafurd wanted him to sign the two-physician agreement required to overrule the patient's right to refuse medications in the first 30 days of treatment. He had pointed out to his colleague that the commitment laws in Washington were very clear that there must be a likelihood of serious harm if one failed to medicate, and that there were no alternative treatments less intrusive than medication that might instead serve the person's best interest. Stegmeyer knew the literature well, including the fact that some patients had been shown to recover better without medication in a supportive milieu. Maybe Alex was in that group. He secretly hoped so.

Dr. Ruthafurd had come again to Stegmeyer's office just yesterday, shouting, "It would be a cold day in hell before I would have anything to do with a consultant suggesting that there were psychotherapy interventions to be made, or even worse that this was some type of 'witchdoctor calling'!" Stegmeyer had been able to calm Dick by letting him know that he would back his petitioning the court for a 90-day hold on Alex and would agree to sign the two-physician agreement at that time. That seemed to stem the tide, at least until after his meeting this morning with Dr. Thomas Harper. The voice of his administrative assistant coming over his phone intercom pulled him from the window and his worried musings.

"Dr. Stegmeyer," she said. "Kirima Holder and Dr. Harper are here to see you."

"Thank you, Betty. Please send them right in," he replied, taking a deep breath while rising to greet them.

❧

As Kirima and I entered the office through the door opened by his administrative assistant, a smile immediately crossed my face; with one quick glance around his office, I knew Paul Stegmeyer and I would get along quite nicely. There on his overstuffed bookshelves sat the same bust of Freud that I had used as a bookend for the last 25 years. A quick perusal of his books showed the collected works of both Freud and Jung, the writings of Yalom, Bronowski's *The Ascent of Man*, and to my great and pleasant surprise, my favorite psychoanalytic novelist, the late Allen Wheelis.

Stegmeyer was a tall, rail thin, yet handsome man, with graying temples fitting a late fifties age range. He sported a short-cropped and prematurely whitened beard with wire-rim glasses perched on his beaklike nose. Dressed casually in a gray cardigan sweater, a loosened tie, and Docker slacks, he added to his informal style a pair of Nike running shoes that, along with photography on the walls, betrayed a still avid marathoner.

He crossed the room quickly, took Kirima's hand, and with a warm smile and a genuine welcoming tone, said, "Ms. Holder, it's good to see you again." Yes, I was going to get along with him just fine.

"To you also, Dr. Stegmeyer," Kirima said. "I continue to appreciate all you are trying to do for Alignak." Turning quickly toward me, she then added, "And this is Dr. Thomas Harper, the Jungian analyst from Chicago I have been telling you about."

"A pleasure, Dr. Harper," he said. "Is it okay if we drop the formality? I would love it if you would just call me Paul and I could call you Tom."

"That suits me well, Paul," I said, while shaking his outstretched hand. "Bill McIntyre predicted we may have a few things in common, and I see you have C.G.'s tomes dotting your shelves."

"A brilliant man and sadly underappreciated in current psychiatric teachings," Stegmeyer responded.

"I couldn't agree more," I replied. "But you know what got me more excited are your copies of *The Desert* and *The Illusionless Man* by Wheelis. Very few of my peers have even heard of him, let alone read him."

"How wonderful that you know Wheelis. I love his wit and the way he embeds his psychotherapeutic teachings in story," Dr. Stegmeyer said enthusiastically.

"A topic near and dear to my heart. I see many late-night discussions may lie ahead for us."

"Well, I'm thrilled to see that the two of you have hit it off so well," Kirima said, breaking into the author critique with a laugh. "I think that portends good things for Alignak's treatment, and speaking of him, I'm going to go visit the ward while you continue your discussions. Tom, I'll touch base later to see what your impressions are of Alignak after you have had a chance to see him this morning."

"Ms. Holder, if you could wait on the ward after you see Alignak, that would be helpful," Dr. Stegmeyer said. "Tom and I will talk for a few minutes, then come over to the unit. I think it would be beneficial for you to introduce him personally for their first meeting. Would that be okay with you?"

"I would also prefer that, if possible, Kirima," I quickly added.

"That's a great idea. I just thought the two of you might be talking for hours, given how you were both heading off down 'book literature lane,'" she said. We all smiled, knowing how true that may have been and agreed to join her no later than 30 minutes from now. Walking out the office door, she turned back with a look that clearly said to us both, "I expect you to follow through."

"Tom, have a seat and let's talk about what you are hoping for in coming to Harborview to see Alignak and a little bit about your beliefs and mine regarding schizophrenia and psychosis," Dr. Stegmeyer suggested.

"Love to, Paul," I responded. "You start. I'm sure you must feel like

I am invading your territory, and I certainly don't want to come in like the Lone Ranger and make everyone else the bad guy."

"That's good to hear. I know that Dr. Ruthafurd, the head psychiatrist on the unit, is feeling strongly about this being the dynamic that's occurring. He's also concerned about the split going on between staff taking sides about what is the right treatment approach with Alignak. I would like to deal with this directly by having a meeting with all treating staff and you and me and define clearly the roles and plans for care while you are involved."

"Couldn't agree more," I quickly replied. "Unprocessed feelings and information floating in a milieu are usually picked up by psychotic patients, and then typically their symptoms and behaviors are exacerbated without anyone understanding why."

Nodding his head, he said, "I have seen the same process occur many times over the years." He then smiled and continued, "Changing subject to the more personal, I trained at Menninger at about the same time you were in residency, given our appearance."

"I would guess that you're right. I was at Medical College of Wisconsin in the early eighties, but I think by the look of the marathoning pictures on the wall, you have kept a little more fit than my current state of physical conditioning," I replied with a chuckle.

"I don't know if my knees would agree with you," he replied, his face wincing while reaching down and unconsciously rubbing them both. "But I was right about our time in school; you and I share the same training zeitgeist. The time of long inpatient treatments, psychodynamic thinking, requirements to have your own therapy experience while in training, and the strong influences of Szasz, Laing, Fromm, Jung, Freud, Sullivan, and certainly in my case, Menninger. I can still remember one of my professors quoting old Karl when the residents on his rotation were sure that a patient, who was just admitted to the ward with a diagnosis of paranoid schizophrenia, would have a poor prognosis and be hopeless for any chance of improvement. He turned to all of us and said, 'Dr. Menninger told me of the first time he began to think more heretically "of the possibility of reversibility in mental illness, that perhaps schizophrenia was not so malignant as we thought but a process that might in some instances be reversible'" (Menninger, 1963, p. 4). My professor then added, 'Those were radical thoughts for those days. Mental illness was not supposed to go away.'" Dr. Stegmeyer paused and took a breath. "Dr. Menninger was considering those possibilities as early as 1922, and shockingly they are still considered radical in our profession almost one hundred years later."

"That is a powerful and all too sadly true statement," I replied. "To some degree that quote encapsulates the essence of why I am here. I have had a special interest in psychosis since my residency days, and over the years treated quite a few patients experiencing extreme states of consciousness using depth-oriented psychotherapy, with and without medication. I believe there is a group of patients, maybe more than we think, that can get, as Dr. Menninger has been so famously quoted as saying, 'Weller than well' (Menninger, 1963, p. 406). I believe that Alignak, from his mother's description, is very likely one of those patients. In his instance there is also the possibility of a calling from his tribal roots, or as Jung would have said, an initiation by the unconscious toward individuation. I believe with Jung 'that there is in the psyche a process that seeks its own goal independently of external factors'" (Jung, 1968, p. 5).

"Well, that has been the ongoing rub for years, right? Is it more nature or more nurture?" Stegmeyer said. "That's why I gravitated toward the biopsychosocial model that George Engel pioneered, as it was the most well rounded and heuristic of treatment orientations. But as I'm sure you know, in this current 'age of the brain,' the *BIO* part of that word is now in capitals while all the other letters now require a microscope even to be seen and considered, especially when it comes to psychosis and hospital-based treatment. We are required to treat patients quickly, with medication first and foremost, because the pressure from the hospital administration to comply with DRGs or diagnosis-related groups is always at our throats. I don't know if you were still working inpatient treatment when this started, but it now influences all our treatment decisions. It basically is 'any of the payment categories that are used to classify patients and especially Medicare patients for the purpose of reimbursing hospitals for each case in a given category with a fixed fee regardless of the actual costs incurred'" (Merriam-Webster, 2017).

"Sounds like you're hoping for a little more capitalization choice in the *psycho* and *social* parts of Engel's model," I said, enjoying his alphabetical metaphor. "Have you thought about incorporating Kane's NAVIGATE program here at Harborview?"

"I am working on it," Stegmeyer replied. But before he could continue further, I interrupted with a question.

"The 'age of the brain'—wasn't that the 1990s slogan of NIMH in their advertising campaign?" I asked. Paul nodded yes. "Let me give you some interesting facts and Jung quotes that speak to the fixed dogma of scientific thinking on this subject, with similarities to Dr. Menninger's musings in 1922. In 1908 Jung wrote a paper for a lecture in Zurich titled 'The Content of the Psychoses,' and then again in 1919 he delivered a paper with similar conclusions to the Royal Society of Medicine in London called 'On the Problem of Psychogenesis in Mental Illness.' In both instances he states that the axiom of the day is that 'mental diseases are diseases of the brain,' and that is the flag being flown by all alienists (Jung, 1960, p. 159). He went on to say that the journals were all about autopsies of the brain and filled with descriptions of deteriorating fibers caused by the disease. 'Psychiatry,' he claimed, 'has been charged with gross materialism...putting the organ, the instrument, above the function.... Function has become the appendage of its organ, the psyche the appendage of the brain.... *Modern psychiatry behaves like someone who thinks he can decipher the meaning and purpose of a building by a mineralogical analysis of its stones*' (Jung, 1960, p. 160, italics added). He then added statistics from that time, showing it was rare in any case of schizophrenia, no matter how chronic, to find anatomical brain changes on autopsy. In his opinion this proved 'that the purely anatomical approach of modern psychiatry leads—to put it mildly—only very indirectly to the goal, which is the understanding of the psychic disturbance.... The way to a psychiatry of the future, which is to come to grips with the essence of the matter, is therefore clearly marked out: *it can only be by way of psychology*' (Jung, 1960, p. 162, italics added). This dogma, he finished saying, 'can only lead to an absolute sterility [of thought and research] as soon as it is assumed to be generally valid' (Jung, 1960, p. 155). How could it be that statements by Menninger and Jung can be just as cogent one hundred years later?" I asked, shaking my head. "We could change the cover from a 1919 journal, give it a 2016 date, put in references to MRIs and PET scans instead of brain autopsies, and include the words 'mental illnesses are diseases of the brain,' and no one would know the difference!"

Paul also shook his head, saying, "Carl Gustav said that back in 1908? Amazing! As I said to you earlier, his work is badly underappreciated."

Paul then said, "Listen, I want to comment on one last thing before we head over to the ward to meet Ms. Holder and Alignak. We have one week, just seven days, before we take Alignak to court on his last day of the 14-day hold. No matter how much I agree with you about the need for more encompassing treatment models and also our current limitations, he is refusing to eat, losing weight, appearing psychotic, and therefore gravely disabled. So you have exactly six days to reach him and to get Dr. Ruthafurd to agree to drop the hold. That is not negotiable!"

"Paul, I have no issue with that whatsoever," I responded. "That seems completely fair. My only request is that I be able to work with Alignak however I want. Sometimes creativity is key to reaching someone in these states. Also, given your expertise and your interest in the wider range of treatments for psychosis, how is it that someone working for you would be so against this way of approaching treatment?"

"First of all, you can do whatever you deem necessary in the treatment of Alignak but take him off the ward while he is on a court hold. I'm also going to assign a fourth-year resident to you. His name is Jack Mullman, and he has an interest in Jungian thought and is pursuing his own analysis at the moment. I think you will like him. There has been a lot of buzz among the residents about your coming, both for and against, and he is one of the residents that was very curious and excited and came to me personally, requesting that he spend time with you. Does that sound okay?" I nodded yes.

"As far as Dr. Ruthafurd goes, he is a very good psychiatrist and knows his pharmacology and diagnostics well. He is part of a young and bright staff that is oriented to medication with little interest or training in psychodynamics. As you and I agreed earlier, this fits with the theories du jour and the influences on training that therapists, nurses, and doctors receive in school, especially when it comes to psychoses. And as I am sure you have experienced, most psychiatrists believe this is a closed conversation insofar as etiology and treatment are concerned. My goal is to slowly bring in more of the emerging literature and mix it with the wisdom from the past that we were discussing and hopefully start a more progressive unit. I can imagine an old-style therapeutic milieu, set up like T. F. Main's or in keeping with Harry Wilmer's ideas, that would fit for these first-break psychotic patients quite nicely."

"A wonderful vision, Paul," I replied. "Let me know if I can do anything to help with this in the future."

"You can do something right now," he said with a laugh. "You can get this kid out of his stupor, and some doubters might start to believe that in selected cases something other than medication can work!"

"All right! I can see there is going to be no pressure on me this week," I said facetiously.

"Let's go get started." Paul looked at his watch. "Good, we are going to make it a couple of minutes inside Kirima's deadline. I would like to introduce you to the staff and to your resident. You are considered a consulting psychiatrist from out of town. You can recommend but not prescribe in Washington, and Dr. Ruthafurd remains the physician of record."

"My understanding exactly."

ॐ

The click of Ward 5-West's door could be heard closing behind us, and instantly I felt the long-forgotten chill of a locked psychiatric unit. It had been 25 years since I was the head psychiatrist of a therapeutic milieu–style unit in a county mental hospital. Now I was entering one of the three teaching units run by Dr. Stegmeyer and staffed by junior faculty, psychiatric residents, and fourth-year medical students from the University of Washington. This was a classic psychiatric facility with a large community room as its centerpiece, furnished with tables and lounge chairs for meetings, meals, and television. Each room had two beds, with a small bathroom and shower. There were three inter-view rooms and another for blood draws and intermuscular injections. There was also the ever-present restraint room with a bed bolted to the floor, leather straps lashed to the frame, and a small observation window in the door. The students, social workers, nurses, and doctors sat behind a counter at the front of the ward or in a glass-windowed charting station just to its rear. The ward could accommodate 19 pa-tients, and many could be seen milling around the community space or watching TV, while another seven to eight patients were in the midst of an apparent group activity in the large conference area.

Suddenly a woman came running from her bedroom, screaming, "Snakes, snakes under my bed. You put them there. You have to get them out." One of the nurses said she would help and walked her back to her room. Paul smiled at me as he led us toward the charting area and said, "Like old times, eh, Tom?"

I smiled back at him, shaking my head, when at that same moment, just to my right, I caught my first glimpse of Alignak. He was sitting in the community room, over in the corner, as his mother had described, on his haunches in the middle of a table, with four other tables organ-ized around him, and Alignak seated exactly at their center. It clearly had the appearance of a makeshift mandala, and I catalogued that in my memory for future reference.

He was unshaven and most likely dressed in the same jeans and University of Washington athletic department T-shirt he had been wearing when he arrived on the ward over a week ago. Even with his hair disheveled and his beard unkempt, it was still easy to see the outline of a handsome young man in his early twenties, lithe and athletic, having clearly inherited his mother's looks. I then looked to see if Kirima was nearby, but instead saw her in one of the windowed interview rooms, having what seemed to be an animated conversation with two men, one slightly older than the other. It was then that Paul also noticed them in the room and asked me to wait while he went over to see what was taking place. A few minutes later he waved me over to come join them as Kirima left and walked toward me.

"Kirima, what's going on?" I asked, seeing she was clearly upset.

"They are quite annoyed that Alignak moved all the tables in the middle of the night, and when they tried to move them back for breakfast, he wouldn't let them," she said, her lips pursed and eyes glinting with anger. "They said he became threatening, but I'm not sure how. Dr. Ruthafurd told me they will not tolerate this, and if he becomes threatening, they are allowed to use medication against his will. He kept saying I am harming my son because of something called DUP, and that by putting off treatment, significantly increasing his chances of having untreatable and chronic schizophrenia. Am I doing that, Dr. Harper? Am I making a mistake by preventing him from receiving treatment, based on my great father's words? I can hear the critical voice of my husband screaming at me that it's all just tribal and mythic nonsense. Dr. Ruthafurd even said my great father was probably a compensated schizophrenic and that this illness is genetic and runs in our family."

"That's absurd!" I said, stunned that Dr. Ruthafurd could be so cold and uncaring. I calmed my rising irritation by trying to imagine his side, realizing he must feel frustrated and helpless by how the case was transpiring and perhaps questioned his decision making. I touched her shoulder and said, "None of that is true, Kirima. You are following the right path for both you and your son. Don't let yourself doubt it."

"Thank you, Dr. Harper. This is just so hard and at times overwhelming. I want my old Alignak back and worry that I may be doing the wrong thing."

"I understand. Let me go in and meet with Paul and the other doctors, and then I'll come out with you and get introduced to Alignak." Kirima walked over to be with her son, and I entered the conference room to meet members of the staff.

Paul stood as I walked into the room and began to introduce me to the treating physicians, Richard Ruthafurd and his resident, Bill Walkner; the ward psychologist, Dr. Samantha Coleman; the head nurse, Jackie Blyther; and finally Jack Mullman, the fourth-year resident who would be working with me. The atmosphere was thick, as the tense discussion that had occurred with Kirima just minutes before even now lingered in the air; yet the civility of handshakes still took place and the chorus "glad to meet you" echoed throughout the room. Dr. Ruthafurd, however, was clearly not glad to meet me and let this be known right away.

"Dr. Harper, what kind of physician would come and lead a mother on by promising some intervention with her psychotic son that prevents him from having the evidence-based treatment that is called for by modern science and research?" Ruthafurd said with palpable antipathy.

"Dick, plea—"

"No, it's okay, Paul!" I interjected. "Let's get what everyone is thinking out in the room right now. I couldn't agree more with Dr. Ruthafurd, and I'm sure that not only he but everyone here is concerned that I may be a quack peddling the latest vitamin therapy for acute psychosis. So let me tell you a little bit about myself, and then we can get everything out in the open. I am board certified and on the staff at the University of Chicago. I am also a Jungian analyst and have always had a special interest in psychosis and extreme states of consciousness, working with many patients in psychotic states with and without medication in my 25-plus-year career. I'm very familiar with the literature on duration of untreated psychosis, as was brought up with Ms. Holder, and know that Alignak's was basically an acute onset, starting about three-and-a-half weeks ago. We are still very much inside the 90-day marker after which it becomes more dangerous, according to the research (Bertolote & McGorry, 2005, pp. 116–119).

"I'm also sure you're familiar with the hypothesis that a toxin may occur in the brain the longer a psychotic break remains active, again placing the patient in a worse long-term prognostic category. However, this is not proven or backed up by written case studies of recovery, even after long-term psychosis, with Anton Boisen's case and the research of Martin Harrow being great examples (Harrow, Jobe, & Faull, 2012, pp. 1–11). Lastly, I would add that there is well-documented research of patients that, when treated with antipsychotics during their first break, do much worse in the long run and possibly are then consigned to poor recovery (Carpenter, 1977, pp. 14–20; Rappaport, Hopkins, Hall, Belleza, & Silverman, 1978, pp. 100–111; Bola & Mosher, 2003, pp. 219–229). I believe Alignak is in that category and, given his cultural history, possibly in the category of a calling to a more shamanic relationship to his unconscious. Lastly, I won't make any effort to block sending Alignak to court if I cannot reach him in the next six days with the minimal goal of getting him to the point that he does not qualify for grave disability."

"If he is discharged in the next week, where will he go from here?" Dr. Coleman asked.

"His mother and I will take him to the Inupiat community where she grew up," I responded.

Disapproval quickly emanated from the shocked facial expressions and headshakes of the two treating physicians present, and at almost that same instant they rose in unison from their chairs, with Dr. Ruthafurd angrily saying, "You can tell us about your fancy credentials, but if your end goal is to remove him from evidence-based care, you are still a charlatan in my book and I will not be involved in what I consider malpractice." With that, he and his resident left the meeting, Paul Stegmeyer following close behind. Voices raised quickly and heatedly, before they could close the door to the other interview room. A few minutes later Dr. Stegmeyer returned, his face still flushed from the obviously passionate discussion, but with one deep breath his polished director persona was back intact and he spoke to all of us left in the room. "Dr. Ruthafurd and Dr. Walkner have asked to sign off the case for professional reasons. I respect that and have agreed to be the physician of record, along with Dr. Mullman, while Alignak is in

our care. Samantha, Jackie, if either one of you also feels that you cannot be involved in his care any longer, feel free to say so now and there
will be no repercussions."

Jackie was the first to speak up, saying, "Dr. Stegmeyer, you're one
of the foremost experts in the country on treating schizophrenia, and
I have always trusted your judgment. I can see you want to give Dr.
Harper a chance and would never put a patient's care at risk. I will follow whatever you decide on this case."

"Thanks, Jackie," Paul said, and I could see he was deeply touched
by her response. "Dr. Coleman, what about you?"

"Dr. Stegmeyer, as you know I am early in my career and came from
a conservative, biologically oriented research program. But I have, like
Jackie, always respected your knowledge and teaching. I've been reading some of the articles you have been giving the staff to update us
on the treatment of psychosis, including those by Richard Bentall on
CBTp and Yrjo Alanen on need-adapted treatment. They are quite provocative and compelling, and I would love to see what Dr. Harper can
accomplish this next week."

"Thanks, Samantha. I appreciate the votes of confidence. How
about you, Dr. Mullman? Still on board?"

"Can't wait, Dr. Stegmeyer!" Jack replied. "I have wanted this argument between the biological and psychosocial positions to break out
in the open for quite some time. It would allow us to include the equally
reputable research that has typically been consigned to the shadows
of psychiatry and that questions the biological-only position and allows access to other treatment options in selected cases."

"That's great, Jack," Stegmeyer responded. "I too am excited to
talk about this among the residents. Listen, one last thing we need to
talk about. Dr. Harper will have full control over the course of therapy
but will not be writing orders. Any change in orders will come from
me or Dr. Mullman. Also, about the tables that Alignak comman-
deered that brought this argument to a boil, what do we all think
should be done about this?"

"Let's leave them if we can," I said. "It looks to me like he has set up
a mandala or sacred circle for himself. I'm sure it has a deep meaning

for his psyche right now, probably connecting him with the center of the world, which is a common motif in a first-break episode. It could also serve as a temenos, protecting him from evil. I suggest we bring in some extra tables for the other patients."

"Fascinating, Tom, I hadn't noticed that," Stegmeyer said, excited. "I can see that Dr. Mullman is already pulling out his iPad to look up the significance of mandalas. Jack, why don't you give a short presentation on that at morning rounds tomorrow."

"I'd love too, Dr. Stegmeyer."

"Well, this feels like an auspicious start to our treatment," I added. "I'm going out to meet Alignak with his mother and if you would like to come, Jack, that would be good." Jack nodded his agreement.

"Also, Paul, I'm most likely going to come back tonight and sit up with Alignak. I've had some success with that in the past, so if you would let the night staff know I'll be coming in late, that would be appreciated."

"My pleasure! Jackie, could you please write a note for the change of shifts to pass on, so they expect Dr. Harper tonight and not leave him locked out in the hall?" Jackie nodded her okay. Glancing at his watch, Stegmeyer quickly got up from his seat. "Didn't realize it was this late; I have to run to my office for a meeting. Let me know if I can be of any more help today, otherwise I will see you tomorrow to find out how your first meeting went," he said as we all headed back to the community room.

Dr. Mullman and I walked toward Kirima where she sat across from Alignak. He continued to stare straight ahead and apparently was still not speaking to her. She got up as we approached, walking over to us, until she was out of Alignak's earshot. "How did everything go at the meeting? Is it still okay for you to work with Alignak?" Kirima asked, concerned.

"Dr. Ruthafurd and Dr. Walkner have requested to be taken off the case, and Dr. Stegmeyer and Dr. Mullman will take over," I said. "No problem with our work together, and if I am not mistaken, I don't think you've met Jack Mullman. He is a fourth-year resident who will be showing me the ropes and has a burning interest in Jungian thought." They shook hands and both expressed their pleasure at meeting one another.

I glanced over at Alignak, who continued in his trancelike stare. "How is he doing, Kirima? Any change?" I asked.

"He is not speaking at all," she said. "I told him you were coming today, but there was no response that I saw."

"Okay, that's good to know. He is really focused on his internal world. Jack, I want you to sit and observe and save any questions you have for later. One of the things I want you to practice is observing any movements Alignak makes with his body and anything you notice in your body. What I'm looking for is your 'second attention,' or what you usually don't notice. The tiny movements or feelings you might typically dismiss. Try to ask, 'What am I noticing?'—that is your 'first attention'—and then ask, 'What am I not noticing?'—that's your 'second attention.' This is something that needs practice but is crucial to psychological work. I will explain more about this later, but for now know that it is a quick way to find the unconscious."

"Got it, Dr. Harper," Jack replied.

"Kirima, if you can introduce us and then say good-bye and leave the ward, that way I can have him focusing only on me and what I am doing," I requested. "Is that okay with you?"

"Perfect."

"Before we do the meet-up, if you both can help me get this other table," I said. We then moved a table to just outside his constructed circle, facing him and about ten feet away from where he sat.

"Alignak, this is Thomas Harper, the doctor from Chicago I was telling you about, and he is going to help you get out of the hospital and up to our tribal people if you will just talk with him. Please, honey, he can help you. He knows about our great father and believes in our ways. Please talk with him," Kirima said in the voice of a mother pleading for her son's help. But Alignak made no effort to respond. Kirima's shoulders fell heavily and a sad sigh followed as she added, "This is Dr. Mullman, a young psychiatrist who will be helping Dr. Harper.

Okay, I'm going to go. I will be back tomorrow. I love you!" Kirima turned to head out, a tear clearly present on her cheek. It was evident she had been hoping that just by introducing me and talking about her people, Alignak would give some sign of having heard her.

"Kirima, I'll call you later," I said as she shook my hand. She whispered, "Good luck, and thank you."

Just as I was about to get up on the table we had moved, the same woman from earlier in the day came running down the hallway shouting uncontrollably, "The snakes! You didn't get them all. One got in my ear!" A nurse attempted to calm her, but she was having none of that. "Come see," she said. "I am not crazy, there is blood on my pillow. You come see it." The nurse followed her into her room.

I turned to Jack, before getting up on my table perch opposite Alignak. "Jack, do you know that woman at all?"

"Yes, I admitted her just last night. Her name is Darlene, and she is having her first psychotic episode. She was placed on a 72-hour hold," he replied.

"See if Dr. Stegmeyer will let you take over that case," I said. "I have a hunch about her delusions."

"Sure thing, Doc, I'll speak with him on morning rounds."

I was now sitting opposite Alignak. I had wanted to mirror him completely, but my old body wouldn't allow me to sit on my haunches, so I took a cross-legged meditative posture and stared directly across at him. I watched closely as he gazed straight ahead, his eyes barely open, small slits with an intense feel and focus. His hands were on his knees and his body had the look of a tightly wound spring, ready at any second to uncoil. He was in a world that was all his own, and my job was to penetrate it. I remembered the thoughts of John Perceval, a man who had undergone a psychotic break in 1830, documented in his incredible book *Perceval's Narrative*, edited by Gregory Bateson. Once he was able to reflect about what had been crucial in allowing him to escape his psychosis, he expressed these thoughts, "[F]irst and foremost...it is the task or duty of the physician or of those who love the patient to understand. The patient's utterance is not to be brushed off as crazy nor is his behavior to be penalized with cold tubs and man-acles" (Perceval, 1961, p. viii). The best way for me to begin this work of understanding in Alignak's case, I thought, was to stay close to what was happening in the moment-to-moment sensory channels. "Stick to the image," as my first analyst would say, quoting one of his Jungian teachers, Raphael Lopez-Pedraza. The image in front of me was of a young man, inner directed but alert and ready to pounce. I chose my first words carefully, attempting to allow him to stay connected to wherever he was in his inner world, but also indicating my support.

"Alignak, whatever you are seeing or feeling or hearing is just right. Follow those experiences wherever they want to go; they are valid exactly as they are. If you want to tell me any of what you see, or feel, or hear, you can, but you can also keep them to yourself, and I will be here only to support you," I said to him in a slow and calming voice.

Suddenly I knew the way to work with Alignak. It was through the crippled man who had petted the black panther in my dream on the plane. I could hear him in my calming voice and now remembered him from the dream saying *sloooow* over and over again. This way of working would be through the body, through the instincts and the here and now of the senses. No quick intellectualized explanations, no brilliant sunlike interpretations, but slow, from the body—his totem animal, the wolf, to my totem animal, the panther.

I sat and stared at him, letting my eyes close slightly, beginning to allow myself to "see" in the dark, just like the great panthers and wolves can as they hunt. In *Psychology and Alchemy,* Jung said that we must facilitate people in "making contact with the psyche," in re-cognizing "the images...lying dormant in their own unconscious." We must "teach people the art of *seeing*" (Jung, 1968, p. 13, italics added). Now I sat with this realization, my energy focused, allowing myself to notice all that I saw and felt and also whatever I could *see.*

Suddenly a fleeting vision: a hand grabbing a throat violently; then gone, impossible to recapture! And what was that? Did I just see Alignak wince? I wasn't sure, but chose to follow these fleeting signals as if they were real.

"Alignak," I said, "stay close to your wolf ally, he is your protector, and let him help you fight the one whose hand would choke out your voice. It is your voice and you have a right to have it." He swallowed as I said this to him and stared at me with an increased intensity as if testing my trustworthiness.

"You're right to look deeply into my soul, to see if you can trust me. The one who would cut off your breath and spirit and take your voice has hurt you. Let yourself take the time and use your instincts to know when you can trust me."

He continued his riveting and penetrating gaze for the longest while. I sat and stared back, saying nothing, both of us unblinking. Then, in a subtle and barely noticeable signal, his eyes closed, for just one or two seconds, but it had the distinct feeling of a nod, of a sense of release, of the possible beginning of something more. I signaled back, shutting my eyes for just a second or two longer, with the tiniest of head bows. We kept on, quietly sitting, but now with a palpable feel of decreased intensity. I could sense that we had accomplished quite a bit for our first meeting together, and it was a good time to end.

"Alignak, thank you for allowing me to be here with you. I will come back later tonight to sit with you again." I bowed to him and got down off the table and walked away toward one of the empty interview rooms with Dr. Mullman.

"Wow, Dr. Harper, that was intense!" Jack said with excitement. "I have a ton of questions. Do you have time now to answer some of them?"

"Certainly, ask away," I replied. "I need to tell you, though, I'm fading from the jet lag and the long flight, so let's not take more than a half hour before I get to go home and crash. I am going to need my energy for tonight's session."

"Definitely," Jack replied. "Okay, so first of all, why come back on the night shift?"

"No special theoretical reason. It is much quieter without the hustle and bustle of the usual daytime ward, so I can sit quietly with him with fewer distractions. Also, it's the time of spirits and animals and the unconscious coming alive. What else do you have for me? My guess is some questions about the words I spoke to Alignak, which related to a sudden and quick vision I had."

"Absolutely, Doc," Mullman said. "I couldn't follow that at all, except that when you said something about the choking hand, I had begun noticing that I was having trouble swallowing. I thought I was just nervous and my throat was dry, but now I realize I might have been picking up concordant countertransference."

"Great job, Jack," I said, excited that he had been that aware. "That's a wonderful example of second attention. You picked up in the proprioceptive channel what I saw in the visual channel, and neither one of us let our conscious cramp turn these experiences into rational 'nothing buts.'

"I also want to point out to you that many things are being accomplished just by sitting quietly with Alignak and asking him to believe in whatever is happening. It allows him to feel understood and supported and prevents panic. But more than that, it validates Jung's belief in constructive or finalistic theory—the idea that the psyche is doing something meaningful to heal itself. Causal ideas are important, but Jung was more interested in what the psyche was doing with its wounds and complexes, not just where they came from. How is it moving toward the future? By my asking him to trust whatever is arising and in whatever channel it arises in, I am helping him to believe that the psyche will lead the way, and we can then work more closely with his individual process and not diagnostic abstractions and generalities."

"I think I understand what you mean," Dr. Mullman said. "So you are trying to have him believe that his psyche is not just sick or pathological, but that what is happening has meaning and its own individual direction?"

"That's it," I replied. "'Image is psyche,' Jung was famous for saying. We want to work by allowing nature to present herself as images that arise in the sensory channels of the patient, in ourselves, or sometimes even in the environment, synchronistically. When we do this, we are helping the patient to connect to their own individual experience of suffering and not the abstractions of science.

"Let me give you an example of this from my practice. I was treating a young woman with severe mood swings, what psychiatry would call bipolar disorder. We treated her with medications with some success, but the breakthrough in her care came when she had these dreams from her psyche and what they had to say about her mood-driven ups and downs. Here is one of her dreams: '*I have just entered a foyer to a home I don't recognize. It has a cathedral ceiling and right in front of me is a small dog, like a wire-haired terrier. He is very wet and the hair on his back is standing straight up on end. He is jumping off the floor, higher and higher each time, now getting all the way to the ceiling. I am afraid of him and begin to back away, but as I do this I back into a huge boa constrictor who coils around my chest and brings me to the ground gasping for air with an overwhelming fear of death.*'"

"That's an amazing dream, Dr. Harper," Jack quickly said. "So the images of the wet dog and the crushing snake are her mania and depression."

"Yes, and she can make a relationship with both of these images or personifications. She can't do that with the abstractions of mania and depression. She can love or hate the dog and the snake because they are her individual images, and they can have reactions toward her. In this instance, too, one can see that the mania is not a defensive reaction to the depression like standard theory would have us believe, but the depression occurs when she backs away from the dog and its leaping, wired-up wetness. In her story the psyche was quite generous and gave another dream hinting how to resolve this problem. She dreamt: '*I am with my therapist and he says we must focus our energy on my dog, who is still quite moist and who is now sitting on a white dryer. I would like to pet the dog, but we are not allowed to pet it or even touch it until it has gone through the procedure of drying.*'

"Now you can see that our goal is to have the therapy proceed completely based on her individual process and images. This is the same thing we are attempting with Alignak. His medical diagnosis is schizophreniform disorder, but that tells us nothing about his psychic world. But the 'choking hand,' as you called it, is our first hint of what might be happening in his inner world, and also the knowledge that in shamanic processes worldwide the initiate often goes to the 'world tree' at the center of the world. There, the shaman-to-be climbs up and down this tree as a ladder, typically going first to the underworld to confront his enemies and demons. That is what I sense is happening now to Alignak, and I am trying to let him know that I won't interfere, but attempt only to provide an understanding and connecting bridge for his journey." I stretched my back and try to fight off a yawn, but Jack could easily see I was fading.

"Doc, let's get you home to some sleep," Mullman said. "I have a lot to think about from what you said and all I saw." Handing me his business card, he added, "I would love to have you call me when you're coming back tonight, if that would be okay with you."

"I'll do that, Jack, love to have you." We shook hands and I went to say good-bye to Jackie Blyther, as she promised to make sure we would be expected by the night shift. I headed off the ward and just for a second I was sure that Alignak had followed me with his gaze!

Weaving my way through the outskirts of Everett where Bill and Connie lived was no easy task, even with Ms. GPS blaring out directions for each upcoming turn. I had always been directionally challenged and had often joked, "Lucky for me psychiatry doesn't require orientational bearings to practice analysis." As she called out, "Turn left at 754 Overton," I finally pulled into the driveway and let out a long and tired sigh. It had been an emotional morning and I was ready for a cold beer, late lunch, and sweet siesta. Bill, Elaine, and Connie all met me at the door, wanting to know how my first meeting had gone and telling me our meal was waiting on the patio. As we all sat down for a delicious lunch of freshly baked bread, Mediterranean salads, and cold IPAs, I began to tell them about my morning at the hospital.

"First, Bill, you were absolutely right about Paul Stegmeyer," I said. "We got along famously as soon as we met, and I'm sure a long-distance friendship is in the offing. As for the other treating doctors, it was quite contentious. They both resigned from the case, claiming that I was unethical in my treatment methods."

"They accused you of being unethical?" Connie asked, quite surprised.

"Actually called me a charlatan, to be exact," I said, smiling.

"You've always had a little trickster in you," Bill said, as everyone laughed. "What about Alignak? How did that go?"

"Well, he is going through a deep and unsettling process, but I thought there were hints that we were beginning to make contact. I'm going to go back tonight and sit with him again. I am hoping that without the daytime ward commotion a deeper connection will be possible."

"And how about your need for sleep?" Elaine jumped in, clearly concerned.

"I thought I would finish my beer and head to bed for a long nap if that wouldn't be too rude," I replied.

"Please, that sounds just right," Connie responded, with Bill and Elaine both nodding their heads.

We sat and talked a while longer, catching up on everyone's morning and the excitement and last-minute preparations for Bill and Connie's trip. England was their first stop, and multiple speaking engagements throughout Europe would follow, with some downtime in Switzerland to hike. But fighting off one last yawn, I finally had to excuse myself and promised to be fresh and ready for a late dinner at their favorite Thai restaurant before I headed back to the hospital. Elaine showed me to our room, and as she told me later, I was asleep and snoring the moment my head hit the pillow.

The ghostly atmosphere could be felt the moment I was opening the broken gate to the sidewalk leading to the crumbling old house. I wasn't sure why I was heading inside, but somehow I felt compelled to do so. I knocked on the front door, the rickety porch creaking beneath my feet. No one answered but the door was cracked open and I went in. I turned on a light and saw broken and uncared-for furniture and then suddenly glimpsed on a far wall a huge painting, eerie and foreboding. A man of enormous size, his face cold and contorted, lifting with both hands to his mouth a struggling human, held in his grip, with unrelenting power, now about to be bitten in half and eaten in the giant's remorseless maw. I was in Goya's house and this was his famous painting of Saturn devouring one of his children. I awoke panicked, sweating, sure I had heard a scream in the far distance.

Just as I was beginning to gather myself, wondering about the dream and why it would be arriving now and with such extreme and brutal imagery, my cell phone rang. I answered it immediately because the caller ID read Harborview Hospital.

"Dr. Harper, it's Jackie Blyther, the head nurse from Ward 5-West. I had to work a double shift because our p.m. charge nurse called in sick at the last minute. So I'm still here on the ward and am calling to tell you how agitated Alignak has become. He had been standing on the tables, when suddenly he let out a bone-chilling scream. This was followed by aggressive growls and now he's sitting once more, but howling over and over again in what can only be described as a forlorn and melancholy sound, like he is experiencing an overwhelming sense of despair and mournfulness."

"Jackie, thank you for calling," I quickly replied. "That's an amazing description of what you are seeing. I'll be there right away, and if possible, try not to make any interventions until I arrive." She agreed, and ending the call I began hurriedly dressing and already dialing Dr. Mullman to meet me at the hospital ASAP.

As I entered the hospital, my mind turned toward the abruptness with which I had left Bill and Connie's house. I had given Elaine a hug on the way out the door, telling her I would call as soon as I could to let her know when I would be home. I asked Bill and Connie to call and tell us how their travels were going, and told Bill I would let him know how Alignak was progressing. All of them had understood and knew how important it was to get back to the ward now that he was making his first substantial sounds in more than a week. As Jackie buzzed me into the locked inpatient unit, I could hear the disconsolate howl she had so accurately described on the phone. Dr. Mullman was already there, and both he and Jackie joined me as we went to see Alignak.

He was sitting in his usual spot, with many of the ward's patients now out of their rooms, having come to the community room to find out what was going on. I took my seat on a table, though this time choosing one that had been arranged as part of his mandala to see if he would allow me to come closer. He gave no indication that this bothered him as he continued to raise his head, howling out his plaintive cry. I sat, for what seemed like minutes, allowing his wailing call to fill my ears and tug at my heart. I thought of my dream of Goya's *Saturn*, the scream I heard at the end, and then remembered the earlier vision of the choking hand. Were they all connected? Was I a conduit for Alignak's process? Spontaneously, I began to howl, with no plan or thought involved, just letting myself feel the immense sadness and grief that was in the field. We continued this wolf's wailing duet for what must have seemed like an eternity to Dr. Mullman and Jackie, as more patients and staff came to observe this unusual site. I heard later that many began to tear up, while some whispered that the doctor had lost his mind.

At first I followed Alignak in the sound and intensity of his wail, but after I felt that he and I were in unison, I initiated a faster rhythm and then a slower one, all the while noticing whether he would follow. He now started to echo each sound that I had just finished making, and as this occurred I attempted to hear the words that might be coming from our depressed melody. As I howled I began to say the word *I*, a wailing "I...I...I...," each word followed by a silent space. This empty space forms a blank access and often the patient's unconscious will fill it. As Alignak and I continued, slowly the words "I...miss you" emerged within his howl. I now added a second blank space after "I miss you," while still maintaining the wailing melody. Slowly we continued, until suddenly the words were clearly sounded, "I...miss you...Father." The howling instantly stopped, his head drooped, shoulders sagged, and a deep deflating sigh fell from his lips. I had been moving closer to him all the while we had been howling, and now we were seated side by side. I placed my arm around his shoulders.

We sat quietly, not moving, until he slowly looked up into my eyes and then in a low but clear voice asked, "Are you a shaman?" As he asked this I heard Jackie gasp and a patient say "Oh my God, Alignak is talking. He's not crazy no more!"

I smiled at Alignak, saying, "No one has ever asked me that. I don't think I am, but I keep having dreams that seem to connect me very deeply to you. Just before coming here tonight I dreamt I saw a giant eat a man and I heard a terrible scream at just that moment."

"You *are* a shaman. I now realize why my mother brought you. You *see* like my mother told me our great father could *see*. I will tell you that your dream vision is true. I met my father in the other world, and he was remorseful for how he had treated me in life and I was remorseful for how I had treated him in death. He said he finally understood and gave me his blessing to follow the calling of my great father's ways, but there was one last thing he must do for me to allow this to happen. It was then I began to growl as I saw the shadow of the 'giant devourer' come up behind him. My father had been possessed by this demon his whole life, and when he died, it had taken his soul and tried to prevent me from becoming myself and having my own voice. When you saw his hand attempting to grab my throat, I knew you might be different from the others who don't see. My great father, as the wise wolf, had taken over my body to protect me, and he bit the 'giant devourer' and caused a bleeding wound. Whenever a demon is wounded and bleeds, all who were possessed are free. This allowed my father's soul to escape and talk to me from his heart, and for just this short while I met my real father for the first time! But now the demon was empty and needed to be fed. My father's soul was free to be reborn, but the demon must take one of us, and if my father refused to sacrifice himself, he would come for me. It was then my father chose to give his soul for mine and you saw this in your vision and heard my scream of sadness."

Alignak took a long breath and continued, "My great father, when he inhabited my body to protect me, came only in his animal form of 'wise wolf.' I therefore couldn't talk in human language but only in wolf-speak. You, Dr. Harper, helped me to find my human voice and climb the 'world tree' back up to the middle realm. Thank you for freeing me and helping me to know that, more than anything, I want to go back to my former life. I don't need to rebel against my father any longer. I don't need to be so full of myself and think I will be a powerful shaman. I just want to go back to my mother and brothers. I want to go back to school and teach religious history. I just want to be Alex, not Alignak!"

I sat for a second, quite stunned by what he was saying. Did he really have this choice? Mircea Eliade says very clearly that many young initiates initially reject the call (Eliade, 2004, p. 23). I also knew from my long treatment of schizophrenic patients that after a "break in consensus reality," numerous patients seal over and go back to their old character structure. Jung called this the "regressive restoration of the persona" (Jung, 1966, p. 163). Was this now happening to Alignak and would he again be only Alex? The mythic parallel to this process occurs in the "Jonah and the whale" story. In this mythic tale Jonah is taken to the underworld, imaged as the night sea journey inside the body of the whale traveling from west to east. In the end he is spit out onto land by the whale with two possible endings. In the first he is naked and tonsured and a great change has occurred in his personality. This would correspond to Dabrowski's positive disintegration, or the idea of the twice-born human. But the second way is also possible, where Jonah is spit out fully clothed, with a full head of hair. No change, no new way of thinking or being, but life returning to the old ego's ways. I decided not to share any of these thoughts with Alignak at this time. Nature and his fate would tell us soon enough whether this choice was even possible for him. My intuition told me it would not be possible and the *irrusik* or inner man that lived in him would shortly come calling.

"I am hungry and tired," Alignak suddenly said. "I'd like to eat and drink and go to bed."

I smiled at him and then turned to Jackie and said, "Do we have anything left over from dinner that we can feed this famished young man?"

"We had some patients that didn't want their food, and we saved it in the break room," Jackie replied. "I'll get it and bring it out for you."

"Thanks, Jackie," I responded. "Alignak, why don't you eat and head to bed and I will see you again in the morning."

"It's Alex, Dr. Harper. Please call me only Alex, and yes, I will see you in the morning. Thank you again."

"My pleasure, Alex," I said and patted him on the shoulder as he began eating the food Jackie placed in front of him like he was now part "starving wolf."

Jackie, Jack Mullman, and I all headed toward one of the interview rooms, and as we entered I was surprised to look out the windows onto the pitch black of the outside world. I glanced at the time, and it was now 10:30 in the evening. I had been with Alignak for hours and yet I would have told you only a short time had passed. I smiled, remembering that this was often my continuing surprise when working with and in altered states. I gave Elaine a quick call to let her know I would be home in about an hour and that things had gone better than expected, though quite surprising.

"Holy Batman, Doc, what the hell happened?" Jack almost shouted, as we all sat down, clearly quite excited.

"I will echo that, Doctor Harper," Jackie quickly added. "I was in tears out there."

"We followed nature and she was kind," I responded. "My unconscious is quite in tune with his for some reason, and therefore my dream helped in understanding what was happening to him in the inner world."

"We could hear his explanation of what had occurred when he began to speak," Jackie said. "I usually think of everything delusional as not real, but that story was so compelling and powerful. It's hard to say it didn't happen just like that!"

"Jackie, we would be fools to disregard his stories. They have been documented down through history, within all cultures, in just this same manner. But minimally, it is true because it is his psychic reality, and as Jung says, psychic reality is real, because the 'the real is what works. The fantasies of the unconscious work—there can be no doubt about that'" (Jung, 2009, p. 260, fn. 15).

"What do you make of him now wanting to be called Alex and not Alignak?" Jack asked. "Does that mean he is well and all the grandiosity of shamanism was just a delusional defense?"

"What does your gut tell you on this question if you continue to think imaginatively and not return to diagnostic abstractions?" I questioned back.

"I can't imagine his great father will not come back quite strongly in his response," Jackie replied, and Jack nodded his head in agreement.

"But that doesn't mean there aren't cases that end tragically, as when patients reject their fate or don't have the courage or power to fight off the demons," I said. "I remember a very important lesson about this that I learned during my early years of practice.

"Years ago I saw an 18-year-old man named Albert in his first psychotic episode. He was transferred from a private hospital, after his insurance ran out, to the county facility where I was working. His was an amazing case and taught me many lessons that even 30 years later I have not forgotten.

"Albert was medicated when I saw him, so he was able to talk about his delusions with a little distance. He had been experiencing homosexual panic that had begun on a camping trip with another friend about the same age. He felt sexual urges toward this young man and then began to experience the wind howling and laughing at him, calling him a queer. Shortly after, he was hospitalized at one of the elite private hospitals in the area. Apparently, at the hospital he was under the care of a psychodynamically oriented psychiatrist who was doing daily therapy with him. He had cleared quite a bit after medication, which is often the case in first breaks. The doctor was interpreting to him that his homoerotic feelings toward the young man were really displaced and latent homoerotic urges toward his father. Albert naturally rejected these interpretations and was not very open to therapy if it was going to head in this direction.

"I agreed with him that this was not a useful way to look at what he was experiencing. I told him I would like to meet with him daily and at that time gather further details about his life. I encouraged him to watch his dreams, saying we would also discuss those. He agreed and told me his first dream the next day. *'I am a little boy and hiding behind a golden chair. I am hanging on tight. My father is coming home soon. I awake.'* He told me he was about four or five in the dream. The golden chair was his mother's favorite. He remembered her sitting in it all the time, knitting. He was close to his mother and was an only child. I mentioned he was holding on tight to the chair, as if he were afraid. 'My dad was scary growing up. My mom and dad were always fighting about him being too hard on me. He thinks I'm a momma's boy,' Albert added with some sadness.

"The first time I met Albert's father helped me to understand his statements. Mr. Crabtree was a smallish man who worked as a business executive, very forceful, extremely opinionated, and always wanting his way. As Albert and I talked more, I was slowly able to gain his confidence, enough to ask about the friend he had the erotic feelings toward. He wanted to tell me, first and foremost, that he was interested in girls. He didn't understand why this had happened. I assured him I understood. He said his friend was a bad boy, real good with the girls, and in trouble a lot in school. Nobody messed with him. He was cool.

"It was clear, though I didn't say it to Albert at the time, that his masculine shadow had been projected onto his friend, a modern Enkidu from the ancient Gilgamesh epic. His psychiatrist at the private hospital wasn't so far off. He had just literalized his interventions, which is often the problem with concretistic interpretations of childhood. The fiction writer's sensibility for the metaphorical is missing. But in this case his psychotic delusion is the actual cure. The symbolic transformation of his libido is imaged as the friend, the erotic pull metaphorically imagined as the longing to embody and have intercourse with this energy. This is the way out of the mother and into his manhood. We talked more subtly about these masculine traits and how he felt about himself. He told me he was not any good with girls and never very good at sports. In fact, he didn't know what he was good at, much to his father's dismay.

"We went on meeting and he continued telling me his dreams. I consider this dream one of the most important teaching moments I have ever had about dreams, psychosis, and being stuck in pathology: *'I am at a swimming pool. The swimming pool is next to the ocean. It is beautiful and sunny. At the bottom of the deep end of the pool there is a small orange juice glass. I dive into the pool and retrieve it. I get out of the pool with the glass in my hand, full of water. I am very proud of what I had accomplished, and then my father comes in. I show him the glass and he knocks it out of my hand and it shatters. Suddenly the scene changes and I am in the parking lot. The cars are all turning into sharks and the grilles into huge aggressive teeth. I awake terrified.'*

"What do you say about a dream like this? The psyche shows exactly his possible cure. A small container, filled with just a little of the *aqua vitae*, the water of life, allowing for an uncomplicated but satisfying existence. But it is not enough for the father, and then comes the disaster of the sharks.

"I tried to talk to Albert regarding this dream, its possible meaning, and about what I saw as things he could do. But the stars weren't aligned favorably. His father thought he was well enough to be signed out of the hospital and that medication was all he needed. No more therapy was the edict. He told me one more dream before leaving the hospital. *'I am walking on a path like the yellow brick road from the Wizard of Oz. I am heading toward a beautiful castle on a hill. The odd thing is that I am in my pajamas and sound asleep. I awake.'*

"One last time I told Albert and his father that more therapy would be important, that I was concerned about everything just sealing over. But these entreaties were to no avail. What happens when he walks toward the castle in his sleep? Is he approaching the golden castle of the mother unconsciously? Without consciousness, is it all just doomed to literalization? The next time I saw Albert was six months later. He was back in the admission ward on a police hold. He had burned his father's house down. I guess the sharks won."

We all sat silently with this tragic story before I broke the quiet, saying, "So this is one of the possibilities that an activation of the unconscious can take. However, I agree with you both that I don't think this is the direction Alignak's case will go, as I too believe the fates will come knocking on his door soon. In the meantime, let's let him enjoy consensus reality again and this middle realm of being human while it lasts, but keep an eye out for where his unconscious is heading. So unless there are other questions, I'm going to head home and see you both in the morning."

But just as we were saying our good-byes and all agreeing that this was one of the most amazing psychotherapeutic experiences any of us had ever had, the snake woman came running from her room once again.

"The snake, it's in my ear. You must get it out, it won't stop talking to me. If we can't get it out, I must kill myself," she screamed and pleaded.

"Jack, where are we on Darlene's case?" I asked.

"I spoke to Dr. Stegmeyer and he was all for me seeing her. I had a short session with her after you left earlier this afternoon, and I told her I would check in with her every day."

Jackie jumped in saying, "Doctors, I would love to hear more, but I need to get to the change-of-shift report so I can get home and come back for my usual work in the morning. What should I tell them about Darlene? Will you see her now?"

"Sure, what the heck," I replied. "Are you up for that Jack before we head home?"

"It would be great to see your interventions with her."

"Okay, bring her into the interview room with us, but before you do grab some drawing paper and crayons or colored pencils and let's have them sitting on the table next to us."

"Why would you do that, Doc?" Jack quickly asked.

"We can't expect nor should we expect patients in an altered reality to communicate only through our primary choice of spoken words. Their world is filled with images and the poetic, and having clay, paint, drawing material, or even the ability to dance and move allows for a much deeper and often meaningful interaction." Jack went to get Darlene, and I quickly called Elaine to tell her I would be later than I first promised.

"Darlene, this is Doctor Harper, my supervisor, and he agreed to come in and talk with you about the snakes," Dr. Mullman told her as she took her seat next to me at the head of the table.

"Hello, Darlene," I said. "I understand a snake is talking with you and living inside your ear. What is this darn snake saying to you?"

"So you believe me!" she quickly responded. "Everybody thinks I'm crazy, but I'm not."

"Darlene, I don't think it is useful to call you names, and I am much more interested in what you're experiencing. Tell me in detail what this snake is saying, and if you can draw it and give us a picture of what he or she looks like, that would be helpful too." She grabbed the drawing materials Jack had brought in and drew a wavy line and began to write words on either side as if it were a mirror and each word were a reflection of the other. She wrote God/Dog, Live/Evil, and then two that didn't match, Right/Wrong.

"The snake says all these things and tells me always to do the wrong thing. It says I am a dog and should fuck like one and that I should do bad things and think bad things. I don't like what it says. I'm a good person and I want the snake to go away. I need an operation on my ear right away," she told us, clearly upset and overwhelmed.

"Darlene, that's incredibly helpful and lets me understand about this snake and ways that we might help," I responded. "Can you also draw me a picture of how this snake looks and where it might be living?" Again she went quickly for the drawing material and drew a snake with a huge black head and body, but then took a yellow crayon and colored yellow streaks of light emanating from the snake's head. She also drew it with its body hanging down from above as if off the ground, with its head speaking into a tunnel that was her ear canal.

"That's a wonderful picture and now I understand even better, Darlene," I said. "I need to know one more thing about you. My guess is that you are a religious woman and follow God and the Bible very closely, is that right?"

"Absolutely, Doctor," she immediately replied. "That's why this is so terrible. I would never disobey God's word and sin like this snake says I should."

"Yes, I believe you," I said. "Here is my suggestion for tonight, and then Dr. Mullman will come talk with you in the morning. I want you to sit on the edge of your bed and ask God what he would do with this snake, and ask him to give you a dream about the solution."

"Okay, I will do that and tell you what God said in the morning." We stood and said good-bye, and I asked her if I could keep the drawings until tomorrow, and she said yes. Jack walked her back to her room and rejoined me in the conference room.

"Jack, tell me a little bit about her history if you could," I asked.

"I got most of the history from her father when he brought her into the emergency room," Jack replied. "She had no previous psychotic history and had been quite functional, though still living at home. She has never used drugs and her toxicology screen was negative. He said about two weeks before bringing her in, she began isolating in her room, and when he walked by he could hear what he thought was her masturbating and then begging for forgiveness in plaintive, guilt-filled prayers. This continued until she began punching herself during the prayer, and it was then he became quite alarmed and brought her to the hospital for admission.

"The father told me that Darlene has always been his favorite. She's the youngest of two daughters. Tragically their mother and his wife died when Darlene was five. Her sister is three years older and moved out many years ago. The older sister has always given him trouble but never his youngest. Darlene has always been there for him. He's disabled and on SSI. Even though she's 22, she still lives at home and gets up daily to go to work and then comes right home at night to cook and care for him."

"That's really helpful," I said. "Now tell me, with that history and what she just showed and told us, what do think might be happening?"

"Well, I'm not sure," Jack said. "She's still living at home at 22 and might be jealous of her sister. She is also conflicted about her sexuality."

"Does she have a boyfriend or is she dating at all?" I asked.

"When I asked her this, she hesitated and blocked and then changed the topic and talked about the snake," Jack said.

"Well, that's a good example of Jung's word association test in action. She is in a complex and has all the responses he talks about in his famous Babette case in his book *The Psychology of Dementia Praecox* (Jung, 2015). It would be good for you to review complex theory and that case in particular and give me a presentation on your findings. You can see here that her conflict has to do with an erotic complex. How could we guess into that from what she drew for us today in session?"

"She was showing that everything was opposites and she was being urged to do everything opposite of what her Christian values and beliefs are. But I don't understand the snake and what it has to do with anything."

"Stick to the image, Jack," I reminded him. "The snake is hanging down as if from a tree, with a dark head and body typical of darkness or the devil. But it also has a golden ring of light around his head. This is often associated with the devil as Lucifer or light bringer. Since her belief system is connected to the Bible, what story do you know where the snake hangs down from above and tempts us but is also considered by theologians to be a *felix culpa* or fortunate sin?"

"Of course, the Garden of Eden story in Genesis," Jack answered.

"That's it. The garden is the world of innocence, and the snake wakes us up to the opposites and the knowledge of good and evil. There is a temptation going on, and my guess would be that she has a lover and feels conflicted about her father and the apparent sin she is committing in her eyes."

"You can see all of that in her delusional ramblings? That's amazing," Jack gushed.

"You will be able to also, as you continue to be open to the psychotic patient's ability to dream while awake. Then you will treat their experiences as dreams that also possibly hint at a meaning or solution. Let's head home for the night, and I will see you about nine o'clock tomorrow morning."

"See you then, Dr. Harper. We had a good day."

"A great day, Jack, an absolutely great day!" I said, raising my hand for a high five as we headed out the door into the Seattle night.

I rose early and was out the door before anyone else was up. When I got home the night before, I said one last good-bye to Bill and Connie, and then Elaine and I talked before bed to arrange for her plans to take the rental car down to Bend to spend the week with our daughter. This made complete sense given all the hours I needed to spend at the hospital. It would be about a seven-hour drive, so we agreed she would leave at nine in the morning since this would be late enough to miss the rush hour traffic but early enough to get there before dark. I told her I would miss her and hoped, given the way things were going, that my work with Alignak might be wrapped up within the week. I could then join her in Bend and maybe even consider heading down to California to see our son.

But for now I was glad to be alone and just wanted to sink into my body as far away from the rigors of patient care as possible. Bill and Connie had given me the loan of their second car while they were away and arranged a visitor's membership at their health club. I was excited about the spinning class and looked forward to a relaxing time in the sauna afterward. The hospital could wait just a little longer than usual this morning for Dr. Harper.

Ms. GPS got me there easily, and it wasn't long before I was sweating to the music of Fatboy Slim and imagining I was racing Lance up the L'Alpe d'Huez. After class I headed straight for the hot rocks and let myself muse about my time with Jack at the hospital yesterday. Here was a gifted young doctor who knew next to nothing about metaphor and symbolism. How could this be and when had this crucial aspect of training disappeared from psychiatry's teaching menu? As I enjoyed the sauna's heat penetrating every pore and the wonderful smell of eucalyptus on the rocks, I remembered the incredible case of Marni from years ago. She was a great example of the healing patients need from a physician with a therapeutic ear, trained to hear the music of simile and metaphor.

I remembered the call from the hospital. "We have a 50-year-old Caucasian female with psychotic depression," the social worker said in a too cheery voice for an early Monday morning. "She still can be delusional, but we have to get her out of the hospital because of the DRGs." They told me she had no previous psychiatric history and was married with two grown children. I hesitantly agreed to work with her because I was not actively seeing overtly psychotic patients any longer in my private practice.

Her first session was memorable. A smallish woman about five-foot-three and approximately 125 pounds, she introduced herself as Marni and told me when I commented on her petiteness that she had been heavy in high school, so her sense of body image was now a source of pride and continuing importance. She dressed in jeans and a cotton blouse and had a contemporary short hairstyle. She was on multiple medications, including an antidepressant, antipsychotic, and low-dose benzodiazepine, and complained that she was oversedated during the day. I told her right away I would lower her daytime dose of Xanax.

Slowly, in a standard history-taking interview, we got to the heart of her recent story. She told me that about four to six weeks earlier she began to think cars were stopping outside her home and taking pictures of her residence. She felt they were police or FBI and that they were also bugging her phone. As she went on, she often stopped and said, "I know this sounds crazy, but it still seems so real." I assured her it was important to hear all the details and that I felt in the end I could help her make sense of her thoughts. This seemed to reassure her and she went on, telling me she thought they were after her for smuggling drugs across the Canadian border. She blushed and said, "I have never done this. I am not a drug addict." She then became more visibly upset and said, "I am quite worried that my husband is in on it. I think he was also bugging my phone. He is a very devout Christian, as I am. I was sure he felt I was sinning and not being a good Christian wife."

We began to talk about her relationship. She said it was great and she loved him very much. He was a quiet man and she was sure that he was bored with her. I asked if she still felt that he was bugging her phone. She denied this but also said she wouldn't be surprised if he was disappointed with her and who she was. She admitted that during the psychosis she had a constant overwhelming sense of guilt. We explored her background history, and there were no incidents of anything similar in the past nor any history of previous treatment.

I decided to make a move in an unusual direction for a first session and began to teach about her delusion. I told her that one way to look at it was as if she were having a waking dream and to view the material as symbolic. We talked about inner versus outer life and questions she might have. She was surprisingly open to this and said she always had believed in dreams and dreamt often. Because of her receptivity I went further and mentioned we could look at the parts of her delusion as a dream. What if the FBI and police were opinions and parts inside her that were against certain other urges, wishes, and wants, and therefore the only way she could bring these into life was through smuggling them across the border. She then might feel bad and guilty about this and afraid her husband would disapprove.

"What does the border of Canada mean?" she asked. I was excited about her curiosity and openness to the apparently odd and irrational. I told her that one way to imagine the border was as an unknown, foreign territory, a place she was not familiar with and not from. I said we could look at this as her unconscious and parts of herself that had been repressed and were not acceptable to herself or her husband. This seemed to make sense, and she was excited about the possibility that what she was going through could have meaning and not just be crazy.

I smiled as I thought about the years we had worked together. She had made wonderful progress and taught me much about the long-term therapy of psychotic process. But the ability to realize there was meaning and purpose in the symbolism was the key; without it she would have been one more case chalked up to faulty chemicals and considered inappropriate for depth psychological treatment.

I climbed reluctantly from my seat on the top bench of the sauna and headed for my locker. A quick glance at my phone showed two messages. One from my wife, telling me she was on the road safely and excited about the trip, with some smiling emojis attached. The other was from the ward at Harborview, and I was sure that wasn't good news. I checked the voice mail and it was Jackie Blyther saying, "Dr. Harper, sorry to call so early. Alignak or Alex is sitting on his bed sobbing and saying over and over he doesn't want to go. He just wants to be Alex. He is asking for you. Thanks." I texted her back and said I would be there within the hour. I jumped in the shower and it occurred to me it might be another long day.

When I arrived on the ward the first person to greet me was Dr. Ruthafurd, waving at me to join him in the interview room where he was sitting with his resident and medical students. I entered with some hesitation, not quite ready for another confrontation this early in the morning.

"Dr. Harper, I wanted to let you know that Dr. Stegmeyer had to fly out of town last evening because of a family emergency. Most likely it will be a week to ten days before he returns. I am now back in charge of Alex Holder's care since I'm covering for Dr. Stegmeyer while he is away. That means Mr. Holder will be going to court this week."

"Well, good morning to you too," I shot back. "I'm sorry to hear the news about Paul. I'm not clear, though, why Jack Mullman can't cover."

"I don't know what the rules are for training in Chicago, but here in Seattle an attending always has the ultimate responsibility for his patients' care and therefore the final say. In this instance that would be me," Ruthafurd said clearly, establishing the new lines of power.

"I'm sure Dr. Stegmeyer would ask you to reconsider sending Alignak to court," I responded.

"He is leaving that completely up to my judgment," Ruthafurd replied. "I can imagine after yesterday you think you're the toast of the ward, with everyone telling stories of your miraculous breakthrough. But you must know there can be spontaneous remissions independent of interventions, so I wouldn't take too much credit. However, this was not a spontaneous remission and what happened only solidifies the reason Mr. Holder needs evidence-based treatment. He went from manic and psychotic with grandiose delusions of power and expansiveness, to today's wailing and moaning depression. It is now clear that he fits criteria for a bipolar I diagnosis with psychotic features and possibly rapid cycling. As hopefully you are aware, the bipolar depressive state is quite dangerous, with a 25–60% suicide attempt rate and a 4–19% successful outcome (Novick, Swartz, & Frank, 2010, pp. 1–9). He is in need of real treatment, and even though you can still try your unproven therapeutic interventions, I will hold him for commitment and start medications on Friday after the court hearing."

"Your position is quite clear, Dr. Ruthafurd," I replied. "I will make every effort to have Alex well enough by Friday that he will not meet criteria for danger to self or others, or for grave disability. So much so that even you, with your blinded vision of psychiatric care, would have to recognize this truth."

"Remember, Dr. Harper, who is in charge," Ruthafurd said, his face now red with anger.

"You have made that abundantly clear," I replied, while turning to leave the room.

I sat on the end of Alex's bed as he bent over sobbing, his head in his hands. Finally he looked up at me and said, "I don't want to go, it's too much for me. Please make him stop!"

I continued to sit quietly with Alex, nodding my hello to Dr. Mullman as he entered the room and took a seat at the small study desk in the corner.

"Whenever you feel ready, Alex, go ahead and tell Dr. Mullman and me the story of what is happening. My guess is that your great father came back to speak with you in visions and dreams."

"I was feeling so strong and alive last night. I ate dinner and went right to bed since I was incredibly tired, but happy to be well again, and fell quickly into a deep sleep. I got up once early in the morning to go to the bathroom and then it started. As I went back to bed, it seemed I almost immediately had this dream: *A wolf sitting and baying at the full moon. It was the biggest moon I have ever seen. Suddenly a voice, I think it was my great father's, saying, 'This is your fate, you must not deny it!'* I awoke frightened and sad and said to myself, 'No, I don't want that life. I don't want that fate.' But then the visions started, strong and powerful. It feels like I am dying, Dr. Harper."

"Tell me the visions, Alex," I requested.

"First, it was an old home, with uncut gray grass, unpainted broken, crooked shutters hanging on beat-up wood siding. I walked up onto the creaky front porch to the front door, which was left partly open. The atmosphere was eerie and ominous and the sky was darkening like a terrible storm was soon to arrive." As it dawned on me what he was describing, a shiver suddenly shot up my spine. The old Goya home from my dream just the night before!

Alex continued, *"As I was about to enter the house a huge shadow of a bird flew above me and it reached down with its talons, ripping at my skin. I cried out but it kept grabbing and ripping into my flesh until some of my ribs began to show.* I then came out of the vision, terribly nauseous, and went to the bathroom and vomited."

"How are you doing now, Alex?" I asked, feeling his fear of the transformation his psyche was bringing.

"This is overwhelming, Doc, especially with the next vision that has been coming and going in waves all morning. In fact, it's coming again now!" Alex said, his voice quavering. He suddenly began to sob, his body wracked with emotion, sitting on the bed rocking, his arms wrapped around himself in attempted comfort.

"Alex, try to describe what is happening if you can."

"I am up above my family. I am looking at them looking at me, but not me, just my body lying in bed. Somehow I have died. My mother and brothers are there grieving over me and I sit above them remorseful, longing, wanting to be in my body and back in the world with them. I want to holler out 'I am here, I love you,' but it won't help, they can't hear me and something keeps tugging at my back, trying to pull me away. I don't want to go." Alex stopped talking and stared straight ahead, tears flowing down his cheeks, and then screamed, "No, no, I won't go. I am Alex!"

"Yes, you don't want to leave the family you love and this everyday world. You don't want to be Alignak, but something is pulling you from behind, to something else. See if you can see what is pulling you," I said. Alex again sat quietly, his face wincing in pain and his back flinching as if something were stabbing at it.

"It's an eagle. A huge, beautiful bald eagle pecking at my back like it was beckoning me and beginning to grab at me with its talons."

"So the bird in the last vision was an eagle that was tearing your flesh," I said. "The eagle is the bird of shamans, and in fact the 'Gilyaks of Siberia have the same word for eagle and shaman, and in Yenisei Ostyaks' lore this magnificent bird was the first shaman' (Halifax, 1982, p. 23). Alex, I know this is immensely frightening, but my experience tells me that this is not an either-or event. It will not be just death to this world and you forever living only in the spirit world of the eagle. You will come back again to the 'middle realm' of human life, but you will be able like your great father to cross the boundaries of many worlds and bring back healings. But the more you fight this call, the more your 'inner man' will demand his wants be faced."

This back and forth went on for most of the next hour, with Alex experiencing paroxysms of tears and sobbing in response to the apparent leaving of this world and family, followed by the ever-tightening grasp of the eagle's talons pulling him toward flight. Suddenly with one last wail of anguish, Alex let go. His head lifted, his eyes closed, his back arched, and a deep breath filled his lungs. He was with the eagle and the spirit world.

"Alex, tell me what is happening," I asked excitedly.

"I am the eagle," Alex said, almost breathless. *"I am soaring toward the sun and then down to the earth. Up and down, moving in a rhythm to gather knowledge from the sky father and bringing that knowing to the people on earth. I now realize this is my way, my calling and duty, like it was the way of my great-great-grandfather. I hear his howl in the distance as 'Wise Wolf.' He is howling my welcome. I am Alignak!"*

No one knew what to say for a minute, not myself, not Dr. Mullman, not Alignak. The experience was so shocking, the resolution so unexpected. Then in a voice now confident and resolute, Alignak broke the silence.

"I need to be discharged as soon as possible, Dr. Harper," he said. "I need to begin my training. I'll call my mother to see when she can make arrangements to get me to the community where she grew up."

"Alignak, sadly it's not quite that easy," I replied. "Dr. Ruthafurd is in charge and he still believes you need medication and more standard treatment. He plans to take you to court on Friday."

"That's crazy, Dr. Harper," Alignak responded, clearly angry. "How can he think that now? I'll talk with him and he'll see it's not necessary." And with that he walked out of the room looking for the doctor.

"Well, as usual, that was amazing," Jack said, as we walked out of the room together, heading for the privacy of an interview room.

"That *was* extraordinary, Jack," I said, still somewhat in shock by this display of the deep unconscious and its autonomy. "I have read about shamanic spirit flights but had never seen one before in my work. Also, I thought it was a big teaching moment when Alignak showed us the difficulty and emotional pain involved whenever the psyche initiates us to a higher self, and the courage it takes to let go of old ways.

"By the way, changing the subject, how is Darlene doing? Have you been able to see her yet this morning?"

"Yes, I saw her first thing. We had a wonderful breakthrough."

"That's exciting, tell me about it."

"She had a dream, and she was excited to say that it was from God. She said *she saw a picture of a figure 8 and that where the lines crossed in the middle is where the devil could get in, and she heard a voice saying, 'This is the solution!' She was sure this couldn't be right and that she had to fix it. She then drew a round circle and said that would be the solution and the figure 8 was God's mistake. The circle would now keep everything out and that God's mistake was that he let the devil in.*

"I then said to her, 'Darlene, it seems that God told you that temptation was part of life and needed to be let in and confronted. Is there some way you have been tempted lately and are refusing to face it and all the guilt and shame you're experiencing? Maybe a man you have fallen in love with and have been afraid to tell your father about?'

"She immediately blushed and turned away, a tear coming quickly to her eye before saying, 'I can't do that to my father, he needs me. I would be just like my sister, disappointing and abandoning him and only thinking of myself.' Then sitting quietly, the tears flowing stronger, she blurted out, 'But I so love Anthony and he loves me. I don't know what to do!'

"Dr. Harper, it was amazing," Jack excitedly said. "We talked for the next hour and she was clear as the proverbial bell, with no evidence of psychotic thinking. We talked about her wants and wishes and the perceived conflict with her father's needs and her belief that expressing her needs would make her just like her sister. We agreed to have her father come for a family session and discuss all of this."

"Incredible, Jack. You were able to make the bridge from the unconscious to the conscious, and it allowed her to walk back over."

"Thank you, Doctor. I would have never known this was even possible without seeing and experiencing your work in the last few days."

Just as Dr. Mullman finished saying this, the interview room door next to us slammed open and Dr. Ruthafurd came walking out, clearly quite agitated. He quickly entered the charting room area and began speaking with Jackie Blyther and his resident, Dr. Walkner. After just a short while in what appeared to be a one-sided conversation, he abruptly left the ward. As Dr. Mullman and I were observing this unusual behavior, Alignak and Kirima knocked on our door and came in.

"Alignak, Kirima, good to see you both," I said as Dr. Mullman seconded my greeting. Kirima rushed quickly across the room and placed me in her most grateful hug.

"Thank you, Dr. Harper, you have given me my son back. I will never be able to thank you enough!" she said.

"It was his courage to face the spirit world that was the key."

"But thank you still."

I turned to Alignak and said, "What happened in your meeting with Dr. Ruthafurd? It didn't look like he left feeling okay with discharging you."

"Something very strange happened," Alignak began to explain. "My mom and I were arguing with him about his intention to take me to court, and he was adamant that he would not change his mind. Mom was becoming more upset with him, and he was beginning to reiterate his position on the craziness of shamans and what was actually, in his opinion, undiagnosed mental illness. It was then I reached over and touched his arm to ask him to not say negative things about our great father and our heritage because it was disrespectful to my mother and me. Suddenly I was flooded with sadness and anxiety as I saw a vision of a young boy, about age five, standing next to a blood-red river with large chunks of the blackest earth flowing throughout. My mother saw my facial expression change and the sadness that had come over me and asked what I had seen. I told them both of my vision. Dr. Ruthafurd suddenly pulled his arm away and gave me the most horrified look, like he was experiencing an overwhelming panic, and then immediately left the room."

"That's exactly how it would happen with my great-grandfather," Kirima added. "He would touch the person on the arm or hand and often a vision would appear. Why do you think Dr. Ruthafurd responded in such a shocked and seemingly frightened manner? He told us, very much like my husband used to say, that Alignak's spirit claims are primitive myths and acknowledging them as true only prevents people from seeking out medicine's more modern methods of treatment."

"I don't know, Kirima, I just don't know," I said, shaking my head.

⤳

I got off the phone with Elaine, telling her I would be in Bend in about 10 days, as soon as I could arrange a flight from Alaska. Kirima, Alignak, and I were all in the car heading for her Inupiat village and the beginning of his shamanic training. I was taking my turn driving while Kirima slept in the back seat. I asked Alignak to read the letter one more time. He gladly obliged.

Dear Alex,

I know receiving this letter from me must be a great surprise. I am sorry I can't say good-bye in person. I wanted to let you know that I called Dr. Mullman to sign the paperwork releasing you from the court hold, and I also called the court to make sure they understood that we would not be pursuing commitment. My hardened position on this matter changed after your vision, when we were talking and you touched my arm. Please let me try to explain.

I have a wonderful five-year-old son named Jordan. He is the love of my life, and my wife recently had been telling me he was coming home from kindergarten complaining of being tired and occasionally short of breath when out for recess. She had taken him to the doctor, and they said it was just a growth spurt and probable seasonal allergies and not to worry. But then you had the vision of the blood river and the black earth and I instantly realized something was terribly wrong with my son. I went home, picked up Jordan and my wife, and we immediately went to the emergency room where they drew his blood. He has leukemia, but a very curable type, and the emergency room doctor said it was fortunate that we were discovering it so early. As I sit in Seattle Children's hospital this morning writing this letter, waiting to meet my son's hematologist, I can't help but see the irony that what I considered your so-called primitive beliefs were what led to the discovery of my son's illness.

I have much to learn about the mysteries of the unconscious, and as my son gets well and I can return to work, I plan to dedicate my life to studying this vast, unfathomable realm. I am humbled and only hope you can forgive me. I will always know you as Alex Holder, but now I am glad to say I know you also as ALIGNAK.

> Wishing you the best in your training,
> Richard Ruthafurd, M.D.

THE ASHLEY MAKER STORY

"**K**URT WAS BESIDE me as usual, dressed in his pencil-tight pants, paisley shirt, and the latest Justin Bieber-wannabe hairstyle. Portlandia cool, he called it. I wasn't really sure why I kept him as a boyfriend; I definitely didn't love him. But he didn't want to paw me all the time either, and that was good, I liked that. Maybe he wasn't really interested in girls, but that was okay too. I was tired of the 'just wanting a fuck' relationship mentality of my previous boy toys. Don't get me wrong, I love to fuck, but a lot of those jock guys had nothing else going on in their orgasm-driven minds. Maybe I kept Kurt because he was odd and so was I. Maybe it was because he liked pushing the envelope and doing wild things, just as we were about to do, as I sat revving the engine of my dad's classic convertible Ford Mustang. 'Maybe I just think too much,' I remember hearing myself say and quickly looked at Kurt, but his attention was elsewhere, his eyes now widening, his face blanching with the oncoming approach of the 7:50 morning train out of Seattle.

"'Ashley, go if you're gonna go!' Kurt screamed. But I waited, just one more second, I wanted that feeling, that rush, that sense that this is what it meant to be truly alive. The engine revved again as I held down the clutch, the back tires squealing, now gaining traction as they painted rubber across the road, shooting the car through the barrier, the train barely missing as it went by, its horn blaring anger and disbelief."

The tightening chest and pounding heart could still surprise her, even after years of telling this story to so many of these professional voyeurs. Her eyes scanned his face and looked for the telltale signs she always found: the surprise, the disappointment, and the hidden wish to scold her for this display of hedonistic recklessness. They all thought themselves experts in hiding these so-called countertransference reactions. But even when she had done the couch gig and the shrink was sitting behind her, she could always spot their real opinion from the sudden pause, the long breath, the increased scribbling on the note pad, and the overintellectualized crafting of their go-to response, "How does telling me that make you feel?"

She had done this therapy thing for years, and it had never made any difference. It always ended up the same. Overflowing bookshelves, expensive leather couches, Persian rugs, and fine artwork, and the words: "You will need to see me two times a week — no, make that three — no, we better make that four and on the couch. Also, this may take years and it will be two hundred dollars a session. Oh, and by the way, do you have good insurance?"

Dr. Thomas Harper sat quietly for the longest time. They were face to face, no couch in his office, just the old wooden rocking chairs they were sitting on. Of course, there were still the obligatory books and diplomas on the wall, but something felt different. Ashley thought, *I feel different! I can't sense the signals that have always accompanied my past therapy visits.* She looked at him more closely.

They have to be here, they always are. He's reasonably good looking for an analyst type: square jaw, graying hair, wavy around the sides of his bald head. He's wearing faded jeans, a black crew neck pullover, scuffed Birkenstocks, and an ill-fitting, too-large-for-him shawl-collar sweater, pulled cozily up around his neck. He looks younger than my girlfriend led me to believe, somewhere in his late fifties, but she told me his website said he was 65. That's my dad's age. Yuck! I already don't like that con-

nection. My girlfriend saw him for years and said he was different from most analysts and had really helped her. She also said he worked with dreams, both those during the night and from within the body, whatever that means, and thought his approach might be useful for me. I'm not so sure. I've done dream work before; it didn't impress me. If I hear one more dream interpretation, telling me about my reaction formation from a distant, intellectual father, compensated by oversexualized and thrill-seeking behavior that is orchestrated by my unconscious need to hide my attachment issues and inner emptiness, I might well go postal. But none of the shrink or shrinkette responses I am so immune to are coming my way. He just continues to sit there, almost meditating. I need to break this silence to find out what's going on in his balding head.

"Dr. Harper, don't you have any response to my story," she said with a tone of reproach.

"I'm sorry," he said smiling. "I got caught in the wonderful memory of that car, my girlfriend and me driving a red '65 Mustang, top down, in the hills of Vermont."

Shocked by his response, but not thinking well on her feet, she replied, "I thought your website said you were married." *What a stupid thing to say,* she thought. *What do I care if he's having a fling?*

"Ah, you're wondering if I am having an affair or am recently divorced. Nothing that spicy to report. That memory is ancient and from old medical school days. I've been married for 31 years with two grown children. But you were wondering also about my response to your story and the questions it stirred in me?"

"Yes," she replied with obvious irritation. "It was such an odd and uncaring direction for you to take in the session. I have had a lot of therapy, some from very well-known and respected analysts, and not one of them ever responded so bizarrely. I was telling you about the reason I came in today for treatment, and that's why I brought up the past story from my high school years. I bring up the painfulness of my compulsion toward danger and flirting with death, and you talk about an old girlfriend and a red convertible!" The fire had returned to her voice, with the sense that she was now back in charge of their encounter.

"That is a fair assessment," he calmly remarked. "Let me take a second to connect to why my reverie and associations went in that direction. Is that okay with you?" Again, she was thrown off guard. He showed no defensiveness, and instead seemed to welcome her challenging comments. She nodded her assent.

Dr. Harper shut his eyes and placed his forehead in his right hand, rubbing it gently as he went deeply within himself. "I can see the winding roads in the hills of Vermont, feel the wind on my face, hear the woman beside me laughing, that exuberant feeling of being in the moment and the vibrant rush of life all around," he reported, opening his eyes and looking directly at her. "Ashley, isn't that what you were looking for when the car shot across the tracks? Vibrancy, energy, life, and a way to truly feel it? Your soul is trying awfully hard to connect with you, in any way it can, no matter how extreme."

She was dumbfounded. *How could he have gotten to my longing, my deepest yearning, so quickly and used my name in such a way that it penetrated me? And how had he done that without asking me, and through some stupid memory from years ago in Vermont? And what about this soul thing? No analyst had ever said that before. I'm not going to let him talk some new age gobbledygook to me.*

"I have had a lot of analysis, Dr. Harper, as I told you earlier, and none of the analysts ever said anything about the soul or that my compulsive behavior could be purposeful. They all told me it's nothing but infantile acting out from my childhood, and all have interpreted issues with my father, my attachment wounds, and with my feelings of emptiness."

"How's that working for you?" he said with a friendly smile.

"You sound like Dr. Phil!" she countered angrily.

"Yes, I stole that line from him," Dr. Harper said laughing. "It's the only good one he has, and other than that I am not sure he is doing the field of psychotherapy many favors. But let me address your concerns about me directly. Ashley, from what you've said, you have come to see me after many years of therapy and experiencing little relief. You can recite all those interpretations by heart, and yet you don't feel any better, more alive, less controlled by your yearning, less driven by your compulsion. The daimon that drives you is still unknown and controlling your life. On that basis I see no benefit to rehashing the same analytic road you have traveled so many times with so little to show for it."

A quiet settled in the room between them. Ashley leaned back in her rocker, taking a deep and calming breath. The session had been so intense from the start that it was only now that he noticed her obvious beauty. She dressed in a gauzy white blouse over a khaki skirt, short enough to show off long, tan, athletic legs. A natural blond, she wore her hair shoulder length, today pulled back in a casual ponytail. A dimple played hide-and-seek on the right side of her face, depending on her smile. But her most arresting feature were her eyes. They were large and the brightest of blues, and for just a moment, he had the feeling he had known Ashley from somewhere in his past. A vague memory, younger, a tattered dress, torn shoes, those same eyes.

"Dr. Harper, you're daydreaming again," Ashley said, bringing him abruptly back to the moment. "Is this going to be the way you conduct my treatment? Because if it is, I'm not sure I like it." Before he could answer, he was aware of one last glimpse of the urchin-like image, now a four- or five-year-old blond girl running away from him in a barren, war-rent city.

"My apologies, I don't mean to be so absentminded-professor-like, and yes and no to your question of how we might do therapy together. No, in that I want to be considerate about our relationship and always let you know that I am not ignoring you and just indulging myself in some inner fantasy world. But yes when it comes to the importance I place on what you just referred to as daydreaming and what I might call instead 'the dreaming.' This can occur anywhere, at any time. Most people encounter it during their nighttime dreams, but it can also occur in the symptoms and signals from your body and during our relationship together, in the space between us. It happened today as you experienced during my reverie from years ago while driving in the mountains, and connected it to the same yearning you felt so profoundly in your story with Kurt."

"I know it did," Ashley said softly. "It was very powerful and some-what disconcerting to have you touch this part of me with words and images that expressed it so accurately and so deeply. I'm not quite sure how to respond. You bring up meaning and purpose but aren't connecting it to my childhood causes, while talking about the soul and demons, as if somehow you're saying I'm possessed."

"Metaphorically, Ashley, the as-if of the dream world," Dr. Harper said to clarify, understanding her confusion. "It is as if you were pos-sessed by what the Greeks might have called a daimon. This differs from a demon in that it can feel negative and controlling, but in the end it can be your greatest gift and strength and connection to your true self."

"But it seems so woo-woo and new agey, like you have taken me to some alternative fragrance bookstore on 23rd Street in Portland," she said, displaying her best sarcastic side. "Don't you adhere to any of the current developmental causal theories of neurosis and character wounding?"

"You have great questions and legitimate concerns," he responded. "I am very familiar with present psychological theory and its focus on development and object relations. I would agree that these stories can be quite helpful at certain times, but as I said earlier, you know all this from your many years of analysis and yet your compulsion is still here, as powerful as ever. But I would also say that the current psychologic-al zeitgeist has eschewed the ages of old and the ancient mythological beliefs that can connect us more powerfully to the actual sense of being possessed by an 'other.' This is what I believe our work can be about, the feeling of connecting you to this 'other' and the future it is pulling you toward."

Ashley shot a glance at the clock, its ticking hands moving ever closer to the therapy profession's "hour," lasting only fifty minutes. There was so much more she wanted to say and ask, but she knew the un-bending rules of the analytic frame quite well. "I see our time is al-most up. My girlfriend was right, you *are* different. I haven't made up my mind whether you can help me or not, but my time today was anything but typical, and I am willing to come back next week and discuss it."

"I'm glad, Ashley. I would like that," Dr. Harper said, "How about this same time next Tuesday, when we can gather more background and see how we might want to work together going forward. Please remember your dreams of the night; they could be quite helpful." She rolled her eyes, but nodded her compliance. "Any other questions before we stop for the day?" he asked, beginning to get up from his chair to open the office door.

"I was curious, if you don't mind, what you were reflecting about during that period of silence in our session," she asked, as she also rose from her rocking chair and began to accept his handshake before leaving.

"I saw a little girl running from me, dressed like she was homeless in a war-torn village. Someone I seemed to know from my past," Dr. Harper responded. But just as the words left his mouth, Ashley was reacting, stepping backward, dropping his hand, a look of shock evident across her face. She sat quickly back into her rocker, her breathing now shallow and rapid, her lips discoloring and pupils dilating. She was having a full-blown panic attack. As he helped to calm her, by deepening and slowing her breath, she was able to gather herself and describe what had just occurred.

"When you were recounting your vision of the little girl, the most horrible feelings of fear and sadness washed over me," Ashley said. "I'm not sure from what, but the dread was like nothing I have ever encountered." She sat for a moment longer, the color returning to her face. He told her that she could take as long as she needed and wondered if they should call someone to come and drive her home. Shaking her head no as she rose from the chair, Ashley said, "I'm better now and fine to drive myself." She took his outstretched hand to shake it good-bye, and as she walked through the office door, turned back slightly for one last comment. "I guess when I said earlier that this was not a typical first session, it may have been a touch understated," she said, a smile playing across her face.

Dr. Harper smiled back and asked her to be careful taking the flight of stairs to the first floor. Watching closely from the top of the steps, he was still stunned by the events at the end of the hour, with no sense of understanding about what had occurred. He listened for the front door to shut behind her before returning to his office, closing the door to take just a minute to collect himself before his next patient arrived.

Suddenly it all came back. The little girl, the tattered dress, the blond hair, the deep-set blue eyes. He remembered now: she had saved him from being killed in a dream he had had years ago, the night after the worst panic attack of his life. The dream showed the world in conflagration, set afire by the Sun God, Apollo, who had come too close to the earth with his chariot. But this same urchin girl had saved him by placing snow on his face and making him invisible to the enemy. What did this have to do with Ashley, and how could his dream have precipitated a panic attack in her, even as it related to his own panic attack?

He heard the bell from the front door ring, indicating his next patient had arrived. He would have to put these questions out of his mind till later; the business executive he was about to see expected his full attention. Walking down the steps to get his patient, he noticed his head shaking while mumbling to himself, "The psyche can be so damn confusing and yet so amazing."

The smell of the Sumatra Dark Roast and the early spring sunlight dancing across the pillow pried her weakening grip from the last remnants of sleep. The dream she awoke in was receding quickly, and struggling to catch it, she reluctantly had to admit she wanted to please her new analyst and knew this was her last chance before their morning session. *Was it a gold-colored kitten she had seen, newly born, being petted by an unknown man?* It made no sense. What was he going to do with this vague, "it couldn't really mean anything" dream? The questions ran nonstop through her mind. Why the panic anxiety at the end of the first session? Could he really help her with that feeling of sadness? Maybe it was just a fluke and she wouldn't feel it again. Maybe she really didn't need therapy after all; nothing useful had ever come from it, though for a second she remembered feeling a vague sense of hope after that first visit.

"Ugh," she said to herself, shaking her head vigorously, hoping, like a dog throwing water off its back, to rid herself of these worthless wishes. *I can't sit around like some little girl waiting to be rescued*, Ashley thought with disdain, now abruptly rolling out of bed for her morning yoga. Assuming her favorite posture to stretch a stiff back, brought on by a long night of horizontal gymnastics, she became aware of the faintest sensation on the top of her head. She reached to touch it, her hand now moving in a tender caress, her head moving to meet her hand as if she were now the cat. A tear slid down her cheek. Feelings of care, of tenderness, of compassion, coursed through her body. Confused, she tried to stand, but a wave of wailing sadness erupted from her mouth and brought her to her knees. It was the same panicky feelings of dread she had felt at Dr. Harper's office.

"What the hell! Ashley, are you okay?" shouted Alex, running to their bedroom from his morning coffee duty in the kitchen.

"I was dreaming of a kitty and then suddenly 'she was me' and I was longing for love and overcome with grief and remorse," she said, her voice quavering with emotion, as she unconsciously reached for his hand.

"Oh, Ashley," Alex responded dismissively, without taking her hand, and turned to head back to the kitchen. "I thought you had broken something and really hurt yourself. Crying over a dream kitten, are you kidding? You don't even like cats. Remember, it was just a dream and anyway you better hurry; we have to get my Land Rover into the shop this morning. They said it wouldn't be available for the weekend kayaking trip if we didn't get it there today. You can follow me to the dealership and then drop me at the office. I have to get some billing done before my meeting with the partners. I think they're going to offer me a junior partnership today. I'll be the youngest in the history of the firm. Pretty impressive! We can celebrate later tonight when I get home. Wear that same sexy thing as last night; that was hot. I'm going to catch a quick shower; your coffee is on the counter." His voice trailed off as the bathroom door shut behind him. *Finally*, she thought, *he's finished talking.*

Still on her knees, confused about the dream and the emotions it had so powerfully precipitated, Ashley also wondered about Alex and why she kept him around. The sex was good, she thought, smiling. He was uninhibited and there were no squishy feelings of attachment. He also liked being on the edge, as did she: downhill skiing on black diamond trails, kayaking the four-plus rapids on the most dangerous line, bungee-jumping off the highest bridges, skydiving and pulling the ripcord at the last second. Even the images brought a feeling of erotic excitement. But he was so damn narcissistic and had no interest in how she felt.

A long-forgotten memory came drifting back. He was driving away. She was begging no. The divorce was final. She was four and dressed in his favorite princess dress with the magical slippers. Her father would never leave if she had that dress on. He had loved that dress and her in it, sweeping her up whenever she wore it. She would stand on his feet with hers as he whirled her around, dancing. What was that song? "I knew ...no ...I know ...yes, yes," she said, nodding. "I know you, I walked with you once upon a dream. I know you, the gleam in your eyes is so familiar...," she sang softly to herself, tears again streaming down her face. It was *The Sleeping Beauty Waltz*, the song he had sung to her when they danced. She felt the memory in her body, as if it were happening now: the turning, the spinning, the whirling, the excitement, and the love of a four-year-old little girl for her father.

Another memory floated by. She was a teenager going through old pictures for a school project. Suddenly there she was, Cinderella-like: dress, slippers, wand in hand, and her biggest toothy smile. She could see the box, down by her feet in the storage closet, right where her mother had left it years ago. She opened it. The wand, with its tin-foil star still glued precariously to the old willow branch, sat atop the yellowed, tattered dress, the torn, moth-riddled slippers by its side. A déjà vu–like feeling was present. Why were long-forgotten memories coming so irresistibly to mind, feelings so familiar and seemingly so important to her life in the moment?

"Ashley, what are you doing?" she heard Alex angrily ask, suddenly standing at the bedroom door dressed in his Ermenegildo Zegna lawyer suit, clearly ready to leave.

"I'm sorry, Alex," she said. "I got caught in some vivid memories from my past. They seem important. You take my car and pick me up later, and we'll make sure we get the Land Rover for the weekend. I'll take a taxi to my analyst this morning at 10. Not a problem."

"Ashley, what is going on?" Alex questioned. "This isn't like you. You haven't been the same since you saw that shrink last week. I thought you said he was a little weird and that we agreed you weren't going to get involved in all that psychobabble again."

"Alex, I did say he was different from the others, but I told you I was going back for at least one more session," she said firmly.

"Okay, Ashley, but remember, all the latest research has shown dreams to be garbage cleanup from the day," Alex retorted. "I have been doing research on a murder case for one of our senior litigators. His wacko client thought his fantasies were the same as reality and then killed somebody because of it. Random neuron firing is what the great scientist Sir Francis Crick calls it; nothing to do with actuality and realism, just garbage collection systems, clearing our brains of worthless thoughts. So don't get caught up emotionally in some silly cat dream; I need you ready to kayak this weekend and to celebrate my partnership tonight. We can pick up the wine on the way home. Okay, gotta run. I'm late." He blew her a half-hearted kiss and was out the door.

She shut her eyes for just a moment more, as a deep, audible sigh filled the room. There was a lot to think about, including whether she wanted to stay in a relationship with a man like Alex. She finally got up from her spot on the floor and headed for the bathroom. There was still plenty of time for a shower and a bite to eat before heading across town for her second appointment with Dr. Harper.

☙

Dr. Harper's 40-minute drive from home to his private practice usually went by quickly. He would usually spend the time reflecting on his dreams, enjoying the play of imagery from the night before, realizing that if he could bring them to consciousness they often gave a hint for what might occur later in therapy. But today was different; he was having trouble recalling any of the images from last night's REM adventures. There was a vague sense of *sitting near water*, but nothing else followed. He knew if he let his attempted dream recall go, it might pop up later unannounced. Instead, he turned his attention to thinking about his workday. He looked forward to Tuesdays because he had just three therapy cases before lunch, then he went to a local community mental health center for the rest of the afternoon to teach medical students at a psychiatry seminar and supervise master-level therapists in psychotherapy.

Besides his analytically oriented dream therapy practice, his other passion had always been teaching. He tried to give a half day a week to this necessary eldership of teaching his soon-to-be-lost craft of dream work. It had become sadly evident to him that modern schools of psychotherapy training taught little in the way of depth psychological methods and nothing about dreams and the imagination. He was excited about the afternoon; he had some creative exercises planned to help therapists appreciate ways of "befriending the dream" and "sticking to the image." He was hoping to convince these young practitioners that there were other ways of preventing the angst of "not knowing" besides the avoidance of asking patients for their dreams or the even more insidious wounding that occurs through having all-too-ready interpretations.

But as he took the exit off the freeway, now just minutes from his office, he realized he was getting ahead of himself. He had his morning patients to concentrate on before any teaching was to be done. He would see Marni at eight and Karen an hour later. They were both in the end stages of long-term therapy, each having come to him suffering serious depression. The work with them had been very rewarding, and he was already beginning to feel the grief of impending good-byes.

His last patient of the morning would also be his newest, Ashley. He had thought of her often during the week and the unusual psychic activation that had occurred in their first session. He wondered, with his lapse in judgment at the end of the hour, which brought on such strong and panic-inducing emotions, whether she would return for her next appointment. He had always worked more openly than most analysts, allowing the images that came upon him to act as a dream door. Then like Lewis Carroll's *Through the Looking Glass*, therapy became a dream: alive, present, and something both he and his patients were free to imagine in. He didn't agree with the typical analytic reliance on theories of concordant and complementary countertransference. This map, though helpful to ease the anxiety that often occurred when treading in unknown territory, more often led away, it seemed to him, from the living dream in the moment. But he knew he had been a little cavalier in sharing the image of the tattered blond girl, especially as an exit line to the hour. If more time had been left in the session to process and let unfold whatever arose, his sharing would have been fine. His mistake had been thinking that the images were all his and had nothing to do with her and the field between them. It was his dream, but somehow, in ways he didn't yet understand, it was hers also.

How could this be? He knew about the latest research on fields and the middle "third" that were constellated between analyst and analysand from his reading in physics and its application in psychoanalytic theory. He was also aware of Jung's ideas on the psychoid unconscious and how it might relativize time. But this dream was from years ago when Ashley might have been only four or five years of age herself.

Memories of that time began to emerge. He was a young psychiatrist, just having entered his analytic training in Chicago, driving home from classes and listening to a lecture on the treatment of pathological narcissism. The lecturer was pedantic and so overly intellectual that it felt as if he were back in college, sitting in one of his advanced calculus classes, where he often found himself rubbing his forehead, trying to comprehend its oxygen-depleting concepts. *Could this lecturer really represent the current ego ideal in analytic circles?* he wondered. *Were his reductive and confining interpretations truly what freed patients from their soul's wounding? Was the love that I had for Jung, which had drawn me to apply for analytic training, now being swallowed down the same theoretical black hole?*

Finally arriving home, agitated from the long drive and the lecture he had been listening to, his wife Elaine greeted him at the door, and seeing his stress suggested they sit and watch some television and talk before bed. But just as they took their seats on the couch, the panic arrived. He rose abruptly, his breath shallowing, his heart thumping, and the frightened question from Elaine followed immediately, "Tom, what's wrong?"

He remembered telling her it was just a panic attack and he already had an inkling as to why it was happening to him now. Calming himself with the same breathing techniques he would apply with Ashley years later, he also used an ancient "Asclepian" dream-incubation method in hopes of capturing a dream to help with the understanding of what had occurred. He remembered Jung saying in his autobiography, *Memories, Dreams, Reflections*, that this was the key when he was in his confrontation with the unconscious; that when one could find the images located in the emotions, find where they had been hidden in the crevices of the affects, it was only then that one could be inwardly calmed and at last reassured.

He pulled up to his usual office parking spot. It was 6:30 and his first patient wasn't until 8:00. He typically came in early to catch up on paperwork, but on this beautiful spring day he decided to sit on his front porch and reflect further on this dream from years past. He shut his eyes and allowed the images to return, now in more detail than during Ashley's first session. *The sun was shooting across the sky, close to the earth, and by this proximity had set the world into a fiery conflagration. Landing on the earth, it had become a chariot with four people in it. The Green Huntsman of Death immediately leapt from his seat in the chariot and was firing arrows from his quiver directly at me. I jumped into a body of water, diving for the bottom with arrows whizzing past my head. Finally I surfaced deep in enemy territory—there was now an army that had come to destroy the world. I had come up next to their power generator and realized I could blow it up, but chose not to. I was now exposed and in full view, fearing that I would be seen and killed by one of the soldiers. Suddenly a Dickensian-like little girl appeared, with a torn and tattered dress and saucerlike blue eyes. She began to rub my face with the whitest of snow. Somehow, even though I was aware my ass was hanging out, I had become invisible.*

A deep sigh, and the sudden realization that his heartbeat had quickened, greeted the memory of the dream's powerful imagery. He had worked this dream for its individual knowledge in his early training with Dr. McIntyre, but now needed to reflect on its possible connections for him and Ashley.

Apollo was the Sun God who drove his chariot daily across the Greek mythic sky, but the dream said that by coming too close to the earth and while landing on it, had now set it ablaze. This sun consciousness was too hot, too bright, too close. Apollo was an archetypal energy, something much greater than the human, that belonged only in the sky realm, not on Earth. The Earth always was code for everyday reality, earthly reality. Suddenly Dr. Harper realized that he had become identified, as had the psychiatric profession, with the ego ideal of the psychiatrist on the lecture tape. But the dream was clear that this identification was deadly and potentially destructive to both him and the world and, of course, Ashley. Those in the profession had become the "far shooters," distancing themselves—above it all like Pentheus on his precarious branch—in order to deliver their bright, intellectual pronouncements and explanations. Analysis had come to worship only Apollo and his love of the intellect and rationality while turning against his half brothers and their beliefs in body, touch, and the irrational.

But the tattered and homeless little girl was the drama's solution.

She, like Dickens's Pip, had been abandoned and uncared for, a street urchin. The dream said she showed the way by rubbing his face with the whitest snow, chilling the overheated conflicts and war of words with the cool play of imagination, the alchemical albedo. In this realm the "I" became invisible, no longer a consciousness of absolutes and bright sureties, but now open to the flow of opposites and the many powers imagined in the soul.

Was Ashley somehow the abandoned girl, wounded by an intellectual father not appreciating her true self? he wondered. *Was I seeing this little girl in Ashley, still in need of a home? Was it also saying that I had not yet fully embraced this child of my dreams and her more imaginative ways, even after these many years? And what did it say about how to conduct the therapy, as obviously an interpretative, classically analytic approach would be doomed to failure?*

Important questions, he thought, glancing at his watch. It was just turning 7:15 and he knew there was time enough before his first patient to try one of his favorite ways of dream work. This would involve the body and was more irrational than the classical association and amplification practices he had just used with the dream. This seemed apropos, given the little girl's calling for more openness to her realm of creativity and the imaginal. He headed toward his office to try this since he didn't want any of the neighbors to wonder what the "crazy" psychiatrist was doing on his front porch this early in the morning.

He stood in his office, closing his eyes, and while holding the dream in his mind, took deep, relaxing breaths to enter a meditative state. After a few minutes he opened his eyes ever so slightly, and with a soft, unfocused gaze, looked around the room to catch whatever wanted to "flirt" with his attention. This method was taught to him by one of his favorite teachers and had theoretical backing in the writings of quantum physics. As he turned his head, allowing himself the freedom to pick up whatever caught his awareness without censoring, he noticed the smallest flash coming from the window facing the front yard. He focused. *Was it a cat I saw?* Suddenly the dream from last night came tumbling back. *I was sitting next to the water I had just been fly-fishing in. I had hooked and caught a cat in the head with my fly. The fly was soft and feathery and was clasped down so that it could not open. The yellow-colored cat could not leave my side and seemed not to want to. It was as if she were destined to be my companion, as she sat regally beside me.*

Surprised by last night's dream returning so abruptly, Dr. Harper almost forgot the goal of the exercise as he, out of habit, began to reflect on the images that had just arisen. But the goal of the "flirt method" is to enact and embody the figures that arise, to enter the flowing river of imagination directly. The flirt was of the cat alone, and therefore he began to let himself sink into the "feeling embodiment" of her. At first he noticed his shoulders make the slightest twitch, stealthily beginning to move as if through a field stalking a mouse. He was being guided by his body, with no preconceptions of where it might lead. These subtle body shiftings and sensations had taken on a life of their own. He was now down on his knees, crouching, feeling the quick and instinctual micro movements of his muscles. His eyes darted to any perceived sound or motion, and then with a sense of safety from prey, suddenly he rose archlike, feeling the sensuous stretching of his back, having spontaneously entered the "cat asana."

Sitting on the floor, not quite having left this state of altered consciousness, he became aware of hearing the words from Yeats's great poem "The Song of the Wandering Aengus" like it was being read to him by the poet himself. "I...caught a little silver trout. When I had laid it on the floor I went to blow the fire a-flame, but something rustled on the floor, and someone called me by my name: It had become a glimmering girl, with apple blossom in her hair, who called me by my name and ran and faded through the brightening air."

Just as had happened to Yeats, Dr. Harper's unconscious was coming to life initially in its animal incarnation, through a metaphor of fishing. His sense was that the cat was the abandoned and uncared-for animal form of the "tattered girl." It appeared as if, through this sensual, instinctive, irrational form of animal knowing, Ashley and he were connected, and that the transformation of both their psyches lay somehow in its power.

The doorbell rang, and he knew his patient had arrived for the first appointment of the day. He would have to put these unusual reflections aside, but as he did, one last thought crept through his mind. Ashley's case seemed like the beginning of the rarest of psychotherapy jewels, a possible transformation of patient and analyst. He was familiar with Jung's four aspects of therapy: confession, elucidation, education, and transformation. In his 34 years of doing therapy, the first three were his daily fare, but deep archetypal transformation, especially of the analyst, was anything but commonplace. He wondered what might occur next in his work with Ashley as he rose to open his office door and head down the stairs to welcome Marni to her appointment.

The Uber driver arrived right on time, and Ashley was surprisingly glad to be carless since she could sit, relax, and think about her upcoming session with Dr. Harper. She felt so vulnerable after this morning's events, and still a little shaky. What was happening to her? Panic attacks, cat dreams, and tears, so many tears—she never cried. She had faced down lions and run from charging elephants in her job as a National Geographic photographer, yet here she was, dwelling on infantile memories that wobbled her knees while also contemplating a relationship breakup with a man that just a few weeks ago was talking marriage. Maybe the breakup wouldn't be that big a deal; she rarely kept a boyfriend around for long. She could always find another by flashing those blue eyes and long legs in a crowded bar—the boys following her home like starving puppies. But she was used to Alex and okay with the fact that he didn't really love her. She knew that, but he liked the same thrills and excitement and having a beautiful girl on his arm. Anyway, he was going to be rich and that would give them lots of money to pursue their adventures. No kids either, that was good. What else was there to want? She was too cynical to think she would ever find love. She hadn't felt it since her father left, but then there was that feeling this morning when she was the kitten with the longing and the reaching out and her hand untaken. Damn, there were those tears again, as her driver pulled up to the office. She paid him the set fee and offered an extra tip if she could take just another minute to collect herself, wiping away any hint of insecurity before heading into her appointment.

⎧⎩

Was that a tear he saw in Ashley's eye? Dr. Harper wondered, as she walked past him into his office, but before he could shut the door and ask, she was already unloading.

"I don't know what happened here the last time, but I don't like it," Ashley began, clearly upset. "I've had one hell of a morning. I woke up in some absurd cat dream then suddenly I am crying and my boyfriend is wondering if I've lost my mind and he's going on about kayaking and partnerships and I'm on the floor reaching out my hand and he won't take it and I'm thinking of Cinderella and my father and dancing and then I am thinking about breaking up with him, I mean Alex, and then I am going to stay with him and then the cab and that reaching and that yearning again and then I'm crying again, like I am now. Damn you!"

Ashley slowly sat forward in her rocker, eyes closed and downcast, the weight of her head falling to the support of her right hand, all the while shaking a disbelieving "no" as she mumbled, "I don't understand. I just don't understand what is happening to me. Damn you!"

As Dr. Harper took his seat opposite Ashley, he could feel his want to hug and rock her as if she were a little girl coming to a parent for protection and support. He knew what was happening and how frightening it can be when the psyche comes alive and demands payment for its realm. Ashley's psyche was expecting more from her and would not let her maintain this one-sided, defended development. Now it was coming to seek its due, and the old ways would no longer suffice. This was an important moment in any analysis, and when it occurred it was crucial to help the patient maintain hope and courage so they wouldn't precipitously drop out or worse yet, panic.

"Ashley, I'm sorry you're going through this," Dr. Harper said.

"You should be," she responded. "I was still okay when I came to see you. I had that danger compulsion but I've had it forever. I could still function, do my job, face anything. But not now! Not after whatever you conjured, like you were some psychic at a carnival with that tattered dress vision." Suddenly Ashley gasped, "Oh my God!"

"What?" Dr. Harper asked, leaning forward. "What did you realize?"

"That's the dress from your vision; I used to wear that dress almost 30 years ago before it was frayed. It was my Cinderella dress and my life was magical and my father loved to dance with me in it and then my mother would tap him on the shoulder to cut in and they would whirl and turn so beautifully. I saw myself this morning wearing it again on the day he left, when the divorce was final. He married the woman he had been having the affair with. She already had two girls and then they had two more of their own. Nothing was ever the same," she said, her voice trailing off. She sat for a moment, rocking, then continued, her words barely audible, "My mother was hospitalized with depression after she tried to kill herself. I found her in all the blood, sprawled across the bed, lifeless, the razor blade still in her hand. I called 911. After she stabilized, the hospital doctors performed shock treatments. Not sure they did anything but leave her blank and spiritless. She's been on medications ever since." Ashley looked up at him, the tears obvious on her face. "Did I say that nothing's ever been the same?" They sat wrapped in a blanket of quiet, for minutes, surrounded by this story of tragedy and pain. Finally Dr. Harper spoke.

"I know this is extremely hard for you and that you are angry with me for stirring up this long forgotten part of your soul," he offered. "But that little girl in the Cinderella dress longs to be cared for and wants to make a relationship with you."

"I don't want to remember her or anything about that time," she said, the words exploding from her mouth. "That was my Disneyland life and it wasn't real. The real part is what happens when you love like that and it is all crushed and taken away. I'll never let that happen again!"

"You can try to continue to repress her," he said. "But 'Cinderella girl,' as we might call her, is attempting to come out and will continue to knock on your door, louder and louder I would guess, and possibly with an increased disturbance in your everyday life if not heeded. Someone ignored often gets angrier and bangs louder until they are heard; but she doesn't have to come so forcibly if you get to know her and make room for what she has to say." He paused, then added, "You said you had a dream of a cat or kitten, there may be a hint there for us."

"I woke to it this morning," she said, slowly regaining her composure. "That's when all hell broke loose with Alex."

"Tell me the dream and some about Alex. You didn't tell me about him the first time you were here."

"I thought it was just a meaningless dream. *It was a little golden kitten, newly born. She was being petted on the top of her head by a man I didn't know.* I went to get out of bed to do my morning yoga, but suddenly when I touched the top of my head I was the kitten, wailing and filled with an uncontrolled longing for love. Alex ran into the room, thinking something terrible had happened to me, but he was so put off when he found out it was just some silly fantasy. I wanted, for just a split second, to have him hold me, but he didn't seem to care and went off to take a shower and get ready for work. I was left alone, and that's when all the memories from the past came flooding back."

Dr. Harper's thoughts whirled in confusion. She had a cat dream and so had he, both from last night. She became the cat and so had he. What was going on in their psyches and how had they become so interconnected? But he knew he needed to collect himself and respond to Ashley, not wanting to repeat the poor timing and technique of the first session.

"Ashley, that is an important dream and very meaningful in helping us to understand what might be happening to you," he said. But as he was about to talk on the importance of first dreams for therapy and their often mapping the direction of the work, he noted the slightest hint of movement of his head and neck toward his left shoulder. Having learned over his years of study and experience that these evanescent sentient signals, though fleeting, can be quite revealing when caught and followed, he decided to tell Ashley want he was noticing.

"Remember in the first session that I told you about the difference between just daydreaming and 'the dreaming.'"

"Yes," she quickly said, "and I thought it was just happening to you again."

"You're right, and I would like to follow the 'dreaming' now and see what it brings up for us. I also had a dream of a cat last night and I think there is something about our work connecting us through the animal body."

"I'm not sure what you mean," she said. "But again, this is not like my usual analytic forays, so why not? What do I do?"

"I have noticed the tiniest movements of my neck and shoulder, and if I follow them and bring them out stronger, then they would start to become like this," he said, slowly beginning to amplify these felt movements and perceptions. Dr. Harper began moving his head toward his left shoulder in a slow stretching, his face softening, and soon it had the unmistakable look of a cat rubbing against something or someone in a wanting caress.

"You look like a cat trying to get petted," Ashley said. "That doesn't seem so revelatory, given what I told you happened to me this morning. Of course I wanted to be loved; that is what all the other analysts have told me and all their transference interpretations were in that same boring key of 'so what's new?' I don't need you to become a cat for that information."

"Touché," Dr. Harper said smiling, enjoying Ashley's witty response. "But what if there was an alternative view? What if instead we could imagine that it is the kitten herself who needs petting and that she receives it specifically from an unknown man. The dream maker could have put you in the dream being caressed and it could have put me as the man doing it, but it didn't. So we must 'stick to the image' and not prematurely jump to past analytic conclusions. This closes the dreaming door and kills the imagined figures or characters before you even get to know them. I would say it's the cat's needs we should focus on and also the unknown someone who is giving it to her. What if we were amenable to these images being alive, here in the present, autonomous and interested in teaching us? What if we were available to a relationship with them and not be so sure they were 'nothing but' allegories from your repressed past?"

"Okay, I'll try to be a little more open to your ideas, especially if they help me to stop crying constantly," she said with a self-effacing chuckle. "What is it you want me to do, move like you were and become a cat?"

"The body awareness channels are always a good place to enter, but this direction has been too debated by us for the moment and won't let the work get beyond the rational critic at this point. Let's go another direction, one that can be just as powerful in honoring the dream. I want you to tell me the dream again, but now completely in the first person. Use all your senses in describing it: sight, hearing, smells, feeling. Describe the dream like you were Flannery O'Connor, painting a paragraph with words."

"That sets the bar awfully high, but okay, here goes." She shut her eyes, took a few deep breaths, and began speaking: *"I am looking at an old man standing across the street from me. He is a smallish man, having the look of a migrant worker, dressed in loose-fitting clothes with dark, tanned, wrinkled skin, made leathery from too many years working the fields in the hot sun. He takes off his sweat-soaked, wide-brimmed hat, wiping his brow, revealing a full head of white hair. He is kneeling down by what looks like an old wooden fruit wagon as the wind swirls dust from the dry and unpaved street. He is seeing something, and reaches down with both hands, the largest and most muscular hands I have ever seen. He is now standing up with a tiny yellow kitten, the hair on its back matted and caked with dirt, its lips dried and cracked as if its mother had abandoned her hours ago without feeding. She is small and appears frail and I can see her face. (I have a feeling it's a she.) The*

old man's huge hands are now cupped around her, and I can just see her
eyes peering over the top of his fingers. She has the biggest brown eyes.
He is stroking the top of her head with his right thumb, softly, tenderly, as
he holds her and she looks at him and then at the world around her."

"Great, that was wonderful. Flannery would be proud. Now stay in
that altered state you have created and let yourself come closer and
look at the kitten's eyes until you feel yourself transit into her and are
seeing through her eyes as her."

Ashley slowly nodded her head to his request, remaining still, her
own eyes closed, concentrating on this inner dream space that she
now was quite fascinated by. It was shocking to her how detailed the
little, barely remembered dream from this morning had become when
she entered it in this way. This was very different from any of her past
therapies' dream analyses.

She returned to the dream. *"I am walking across the street toward*
the old man, but from an angle that prevents him from noticing me. I can
see the kitten's eyes more clearly. They are large, and bulging out of her
small head, while darting to every sight and sound. I am staring at them.
Wow, this is freaky; I am seeing through them. I'm her! I am loving the
tender stroking of my head and feel a calmness flow through my body. I
can see the old man's face looking down at me, lined and weathered. I
am now looking at his eyes looking at me. They are black and deep, like
a well that goes on forever, filled with the waters of compassion. I feel safe
in his huge hands."

Suddenly Ashley's eyes popped open, a look of surprise playing
across her face. "Someone else's hands were reaching to take the kitten. I recognized, even in the dream vision, that they were Alex's hands.
They were so small and the kitten didn't fit in them and she was frightened and the old man turned away protectively."

"What did it feel like to realize that Alex's hands could not contain the kitten and her needs?" Dr. Harper asked.

"So you're saying I should break up with Alex, and that this is how
the past is alive in the present with Alex being equivalent to my father
and not caring for my wounded 'little girl's' love needs?"

"Wow, that was quite the theoretical leap," he replied. "No, I'm asking exactly what I said. How did you feel when his hands were too small to contain the kitten? We know the kitten was frightened and the old man reacted protectively. Stay with the image, not your reductive interpretations. I know that might sound a little brusque and directive on my part, but it is absolutely crucial when working with the images in dreams."

"Okay, let me try again to answer your question. At the moment I saw the hands coming, I was still seeing through the kitten's eyes and could feel her fright. Then I was myself and felt a sadness and the loss of the old man's hands and relief when he pulled the kitten away and protected her."

"Now keep close to these images. How are Alex's hands too small for that kitten's needs and how are the kitten's needs handled in your current relationship with Alex?" He could see by the look on her face that she still didn't quite understand his direction. "You told me that this morning, when you became the kitten, Alex wouldn't or couldn't take your hand. How, in your relationships past and present, have you ignored the kitten's frightened reactions and the old man's hints to protect her?"

"Yes, of course I have feelings and wishes at times in the relationship stemming from how Alex treats me. Who doesn't? But those needs are so infantile. Alex and I like the same things, and anyway I'm not going to find love. I'm not still some four-year-old girl who can wave her makeshift magic wand and then everything turns from pumpkin to carriage. I am now grown up and realistic about what the world offers and what it so easily takes away," Ashley said, her voice cold and resolute.

Dr. Harper sat back in his rocker, feeling the chill that had entered the room with Ashley's comments. He focused on this coldness, knowing that changes in atmosphere always indicated an unconscious figure had arrived unannounced. Sensing a chill across his chest and shoulders, he began to amplify it into a body shiver, when suddenly he saw the cat from his dream sitting beside him, trembling, its face hissing danger and claws pawing the air. There coming toward them was a man, dressed in a black robe, wearing an English judge's bench wig, his hands reaching out menacingly toward the cat.

"Why are you shivering?" Ashley asked. "Are you doing that 'dreaming' thing again?" Dr. Harper nodded, while looking up at the clock to make sure there was still time in the hour to process whatever arose.

"I told you I also had a dream of a cat last night, sitting beside me, and I just saw her tremble as a man dressed as a judge or barrister in Great Britain, with robe and wig, was reaching to grab her, like Alex in your vision."

Ashley sat for a moment in shock, amazed at the continued images that arrived so accurately and seemingly out of nowhere. "I haven't told you yet that my father is a lawyer, like Alex, except that a few years ago he was appointed to the federal appeals court by the President and now is a full-time federal judge. To celebrate that honor, my so-called stepmother gave him a judge's wig from the British courts to go along with the barrister's wig my mother had given him years earlier when he passed the bar. I don't understand, why would that come up now and what does it have to do with what we've been talking about?"

"I believe he entered the room with us when you were talking in such a cold, rational, intellectual, and absolute manner about the kitten and the little girl being 'nothing but' an infantile longing and love being a fairy tale. I believe, to give you my interpretation, that this is what the kitten is so frightened by: not Alex, not your father, though they both have this soul-killing quality. But instead, she is most afraid of this harsh, cold judge that lives both in the world, as its current ideal of maturity, and inside of you, as your believed growth out of childish wishes. It comes so quickly, unconsciously, and attempts to take the life of all the just-born instinctual possibilities. That is what the earthy old man so compassionately tries to protect, keeping this frail beginning alive after her abandonment."

"Dr. Harper," Ashley softly replied. "I want badly to believe what you're saying, but I have thought this way for so long. When my father was still dancing with us, he had not yet graduated from law school.

My mother said he changed when he got his first job in the prosecutor's office. She said he hardened, became less compassionate, more cynical, less fun. He would tell me all the time, when I would be at his house growing up, that the world was cruel and the law was the objective truth that prevented emotional chaos. It was the facts and the rational intellect that allowed society and culture to win out over the maelstrom of rapists, child abusers, murderers, and the passions of the damned. *Lord of the Flies* was his favorite novel and sublimation his favorite theory." She looked intently at her doctor as she finished speaking, tears again forming in her eyes. Then slowly, like a jury's final verdict, her words came flowing from her mouth, "I have become my most deplorable fear; I have become just like my father. Cynical, rational, with no room for love, and worst of all, with this way of being, I am now killing the 'Cinderella girl' that I had been so angry with him for abandoning long ago." She paused. "Please help me change."

"Ashley, I'm moved by your humble insights, and they themselves are the beginning of your change. I also believe that if we set our compass by continuing to listen to and follow as precisely as we can the hints from what Jung called the 'million-year-old man or woman of days,' we won't ever be far off the correct path. For he and she have been experiencing these stories over and over again through the millennia, and it's through your dreams and images and body experiences that they communicate so much more than you and I could ever know."

The session moved on, now taking a typical therapy style, as Ashley shared further feelings and memories about her father and mother. She also related more of the concerns that she had been harboring about Alex but was always too afraid to confront consciously. As the hour drew to its close, Dr. Harper said, "This has been a powerful time together today, and much has come up. Great work for hanging in there with some very difficult material. Keep an eye on your dreams this week, as they have much to comment on."

"I will," Ashley quickly responded. "You're not going to have to convince me again that dreams are not just 'random neuron firings.'"

"Wow, Sir Francis Crick's crazy dream hypothesis. Not many people are familiar with that, Ashley. Where did you hear of it?" She just smiled, as the image of Alex's hands suddenly appeared in her mind's eye, grasping the steering wheel of her car when he would come to pick her up after the session. *They really are too small*, she thought.

She stood and took her doctor's outstretched hand, saying, "I'll see you next Tuesday."

"I look forward to it, Ashley."

She walked through the door to head down the steps, but realized she needed to stop and follow the irrational sensation that seemed to be grabbing her shoulder, as if it wanted her to turn back toward his office. "Dr. Harper, thank you; I just really wanted to say thank you!"

AL DE HALF'S SEPARATE REALITY

YEARS AGO WHEN studying for my psychiatric-specialty board exams and feeling quite nervous, I began reading Freedman, Kaplan, and Sadock's *Comprehensive Textbook of Psychiatry*, the bible of information in the field. After reading the chapter on psychoses, I was anxiously awakened that night by this dream:

I am back at the Milwaukee County Mental Health Center, where I had worked for many years post residency. I call the medical director about an escaped chronic psychotic patient who is planning to murder me. He is finally caught and brought to talk with me. A huge man, slumped over with arms that droop and hang down apelike. He tells me his name is Al de Half (my other half). He looks absolutely enraged with me, saying that I have been reading the wrong books. He pulls out a book and says, "This is my bible." It is A Separate Reality, *Carlos Castaneda's book about don Juan, the Mexican shaman. I tell him I have read it, but he comments sarcastically, "Apparently not very well." He begins showing me a page from the book with eight principles on it, when I awake.*

There are many layers of meaning to this dream. Typically, most dreams are interpreted according to the individual's psychology, but I would like to review this dream through a cultural or 'big dream' perspective, as Jung would often call it. One might say the psyche or soul, represented as Al de Half, tells us that extreme states form a 'separate reality,' and that this seemingly strange reality has its own governing principles. To understand and help people in extreme states of consciousness, we must learn to live these principles ourselves.

What are these eight principles? I woke up before Al filled in the blank spaces, and could not be sure if he was just referring to methods and techniques for working with people in psychotic states. It is my sense, however, that Al de Half was not primarily interested in techniques, but instead was most concerned about the background attitudes and feelings we bring to our work, what Amy and Arnold Mindell have termed *metaskills*. Techniques and methods only become useful after the crucial background beliefs and attitudes are brought to awareness. In this chapter I will attempt to delineate eight of the principles I imagine Al de Half felt were crucial to help souls navigate the sometimes dark shores of his separate world.

1. HERCULES SWORD BE DAMNED

There are many stories of Hercules' adventures, but for my purposes here, I would like to focus on his journey to Hades. As he drops down into the underworld, he finds it hazy, his vision fogged, with only moonlight and mist, nothing clear—certainly not his preferred bright and intelligible light of the sun. As he tries to acclimate to this new and unfamiliar world, two shades (ghosts of the dead) approach him. In a flash Hercules draws his sword and beheads them. No questions, no sense of what they wanted, no relationship.

Hercules responds exactly as one would expect if he had been trained in our current schools of psychotherapy. The heroic ego is still our ideal, capturing new ground from the id, making knowing interpretations and usurping more power and mastery for itself. The schools are all grounded in psychotherapeutic techniques aimed at getting rid of the ghosts (symptoms) that approach us before allowing them any voice of their own. But, even though this may appear to work in the daytime world of neurosis, the world of psychosis is much different. It is bathed in moonlight, and the separations of good and bad, black and white, are not so distinct. Here, lack of clarity and being open to what Keats called "negative capability" are key: the ability to sit in confusion and not reach so quickly for the dividing sword of intellect and explanation, to be open to what Arnold Mindell calls "deep democracy." This allows for the realization that you are not the only ruler of your psychic house and that all inner figures deserve a voice.

2. PANIC CAN BE THE DEADLIEST ENEMY

We can see from this last story that panic leads to Hercules' precipitous reaction toward the shades. Panic is an extreme affective reaction brought on by the sympathetic nervous system responding to an overwhelming fear of the unknown. But what if Hercules could have been with someone encouraging a more understanding attitude toward the contents arising from the unconscious. Jung comments on this same idea in his foreword to John Perry's (1987) book *The Self in Psychotic Process* when he says:

"One should not underrate the disastrous shock which patients undergo when they find themselves assailed by the intrusion of strange contents which they are unable to integrate. The mere fact that they have such ideas isolates them from their fellow men [and women] and exposes them to an irresistible panic, which often marks the outbreak of manifest psychosis. If, on the other hand, they meet with adequate understanding from their physician, they do not fall into panic, because they are still understood by a human being and thus preserved from the disastrous shock of complete isolation."

In R. D. Laing's book *The Politics of Experience*, he wrote a chapter titled "A Ten-Day Voyage." In it, the patient was asked what would have made a difference in his treatment and he responded, "A sheet anchor, the feeling that someone understood" (Laing, 1971, p. 163–164). These ideas of Laing's and Jung's were well tested in the 1970s in facilities such as Diabasis and Soteria House, inpatient alternative-treatment facilities for people in psychotic states. When helpers met acute psychotic experiences (the shades of Hercules) with an attitude of openness and validation, they found that patients often came through these extreme states more rapidly than similar patients treated in more classic psychiatric hospital wards (Mosher, Menn, & Matthews, 1975; Perry, 1974).

3. RANDOM NEURON FIRINGS DO NOT EXIST

I took the phrase "random neuron firings" from Sir Francis Crick, winner of the Nobel Prize for discovering the structure of DNA with James Watson, and who later went on to become a dream researcher after his DNA fame. He implied that dreams were random neuron firings with a purely biological purpose. This theory when applied would make it very hard to validate a person's dreaming experience as psychologically meaningful. Armed with this attitude, psychiatrists can easily compare psychosis to chronic physical illnesses caused by biochemical abnormalities and genetic predispositions. However, no matter how useful the biologic theory has been for science and somatic medicine, and no matter what a patient's genetic and medical history, each person always has a psychology. That means that no matter how difficult to understand, the images and symbols arising still form a possible communication system. I believe in the irreducibility of a person's psychology. This belief allows us to continue to look for new ways to work and communicate with patients in extreme states of consciousness, irrespective of the prevailing biologic theories. The idea that a patient's attitude could affect the long-range outcome of their psychosis was shown in research by Soskis and Bowers in 1969. They found that patients who were interested in how to make sense of their psychotic experiences had a much lower rate of recidivism than did the clients who considered the experiences as "nothing but" part of a biochemical illness.

4. PURPOSE AND MEANING EXIST EVEN IN THE MOST OBSCURE COMMUNICATIONS

⊙

This principle follows Jung's ideas on finality, also known as the constructive or synthetic method. This is the contrasting idea that men and women are not explained adequately by past history alone—Aristotle's *causa efficiens,* or the reductive method. They are also pulled toward the future by personality parts that wish to express themselves and to expand the personality into its total creative potential.

"The psychology of an individual can never be exhaustively explained from himself alone.... [N]o psychological fact can ever be exhaustively explained in terms of causality alone; as a living phenomenon, it is always indissolubly bound up with the continuity of the vital process, so that it is not only something evolved but also continually evolving and creative" (Jung, 1921, p. 430).

Jung's finalistic ideas separated him from the Freudian emphasis on causality, and came to be accepted as the standard among Jungian analysts in regard to neurosis. What many have never realized or accepted is that Jung held these same beliefs in regard to psychosis. In the last paper he delivered late in his life on this topic, he had this to say:

"It is now just about fifty years since I became convinced, through practical experience, that schizophrenic disturbances could be treated and cured by psychological means. I found that, with respect to the treatment, the schizophrenic patient behaves no differently from the neurotic.... I have now, after long practical experience, come to hold the view that the psychogenic causation ...is more probable than the toxic causation" (Jung, 1960, pp. 258, 264).

This attitude of belief in the phenomenology and purpose of the psychic contents of their patients helped distinguish the pioneering work of Jung and later his students John Perry and Arnold Mindell. This attitude is absolutely crucial in working with patients, regardless of how bizarre their statements seem.

I became even more convinced of this after recently seeing a woman with a history of delusions and psychotic thinking in my private practice. Marni had been stable for some time in therapy, but now was presenting again with aspects of paranoia and auditory hallucinations. She told me that she and her husband were on vacation at a mountain resort community when she began getting extremely anxious while at the grocery store. It was as if everyone was looking at her and talking about her. Marni began to avoid shopping and had her husband go instead. She also didn't want to go out to dinner or do any of the social activities they typically loved when on vacation. She began to notice when walking her dog that she heard gunshots and was sure someone was shooting at her. After hearing the gunshots she began to stay in her bedroom and not leave the house.

Her husband called me for an emergency session, and I saw her the next day. We talked about taking these events as if they were dreams and metaphorical imaginings. She had always had a good relationship with me, and we had worked this way earlier in her treatment, but she said it felt so real and actual and that she was sure these incidents couldn't be metaphorical. She was being shot at! I pointed out to her that by choosing not to explore these beliefs as we had in the past and using avoidance to get away from the fear and anxiety, though this could be useful in the moment, in the end it would lead to increased isolation and the shrinking of places she could go.

She agreed that this was what was happening and that her fears and withdrawal were definitely increasing. I reminded her that she and I had always worked following Jung's dictum of "not out, but through." Though still sure all this was "real," she agreed to explore both events as dreams.

Going first into the avoidance of shopping, we set up a mini play in my office. I had her follow the traces and sensations of the body experiences she had felt while shopping and to begin to fill out the character or figure that was trying to arise more precisely. She hunched her shoulders and pulled down into her sweater. She averted her face and wanted to turn away. I had her feel into this character and make an image other than herself of this person. I told her it could be a movie star, fairy-tale figure, or person she knew. She said it looked like a woman that might be homeless, with poorly kept hair, tattered clothes, and holes in her shoes. I had her stand and imagine moving like this woman, and as she did she became hunched over and words came out that said something like, "I am sorry for being here—I'm ashamed. You're all so much better. This is not my place."

Marni was surprised about the depth of the feelings. I said she seemed to be talking to someone, as if apologizing to some other character in the drama. She said it was all the well-to-do people there. This mountain resort was for the rich, and she just didn't belong there. I noted to her that I had never heard her feel this way about their vacation location before. I asked if anything had happened recently. Suddenly she remembered she had been with her mother and some other woman, and Marni had been talking about going to the resort for the weekend when her mother's friend said, "Oh, that is so expensive." Her mother apparently chimed in that Marni and her husband had decided not to live as modestly as she and the friend had done. This left Marni quite embarrassed. I asked her how she felt.

She said, "I was angry, but didn't say anything. It's just like my mother. She takes 'potshots' at me all the time."

Marni was completely unaware that she had spontaneously interpreted the reason and meaning of her hallucinations. I said slowly, "Oh, she takes potshots at you; you mean she sometimes shoots at you with jabs and barbs." She got it immediately and was able to come back and see that these incidents at the resort were connected, like having two dreams back to back on the same night.

This was a breakthrough in the therapy because she was able to see and connect her waking paranoid and hallucinatory experiences to her everyday life and to previous dreams. Marni has recovered completely and has not had further psychotic experiences since those events.

5. DON JUAN'S ALLY OR JACOB'S ANGEL

If you begin with an attitude of purposefulness toward the psyche, then even the frightening images that may appear can become allies for you. I use *ally* as meaning someone or something that may prove useful on

your path. The ally usually arrives in scary disguises such as the paranoid fears of someone breaking into your home, or as auditory hallucinations delivering commands too unbelievable to understand or too
shameful to carry out. This would be like the patient of mine who
heard a voice coming from the kitchen telling him he needed to "sleep
with his mother to be reborn." These are the kind of messages the ally
can send, something confusing and morally corrupt to our day-world
consciousness. But the ally never hands over information free of charge,
as Jacob found in the Bible. The angel must be wrestled with, even to
the point of a broken hip. Or as don Juan says to Carlos:

"When a man is facing the ally, the giver of secrets, he has to mus-
ter up all his courage and grab it before it grabs him, or chase it before
it chases him. The chase must be relentless and then comes the struggle. The man must wrestle the spirit to the ground and keep it there
until it gives him power" (Castenada, cited in Mindell, 1993, p. 114).

In psychological terms we might say the first step involves process-
ing or unfolding the unconscious material, the hallucinations, or the
paranoid fears until a personified figure begins to appear to whom we
can relate. Then the key becomes the *auseinandersetzung*, the having
it out and coming to terms with this figure. This is crucial, in that there
must be someone to deliver the message to. It must be heard. If you do
not translate the message consciously, the ally controls you unconsciously, often acting out its message in literal forms in the day world.

6. AN EAR FOR THE SYMBOLIC

It is one thing to believe in the purpose and meaning of the psyche
when it gives information about your personal life, like a dream image
showing you shaking the "dirty hand of a partner" in an upcoming
business contract agreement when you had gone to bed wondering if
everything was legal. The warning is quite obvious. But what do you
do when the message is not so understandable? Take for instance
these statements from patients I have seen: "It is time to put the blood

in the carriage and take the water to the mouths of the people," or "you must stick the cross in the urine, it is finally the time," or "you must put the evil mind away in a coffin in the center of the ring of fire the temperature of the sun." The language of "the separate reality" is symbolic, and we must practice developing the ear of a poet. People who fall unwillingly into psychosis often lose the ability to hear the metaphor in many of the allies' messages.

One of the first patients I saw as a resident was a young man living with his elderly parents. They brought him for hospitalization because he had become quite paranoid, barricading his door, staring out the window watching for intruders, and hoarding knives under his bed. I admitted him to the teaching ward, but the court released him from the hospital two weeks later because he failed, in their opinion, to meet the criteria for a longer commitment. The patient then promptly refused all further treatment. A few months later he tragically came to my attention again when the police arrested him for murder. He had stabbed a five-year-old boy to death because he thought the boy was an alien invader from outer space and the former patient was protecting the world.

This topic has many unanswered questions in need of research. How do you take these symbolic statements and feed them back to patients so they can hear and live them more usefully in their daily lives? How do you help connect the symbolism to the patient's personal life and emotional core? The main principle to remember is that patients cannot hear the metaphor while in an extreme state of consciousness. The therapist must hold the awareness and be prepared to jump into the emotional caldron with them.

7. A NOSE AND STOMACH FOR THE *PUTREFACTIO*

Psychosis is a state of dissolution; the dissolving of the old personality is occurring. When things dissolve and decay, then they smell: dirty clothing, carious teeth, malignant emotional disorganization, contorted postures, regressed behaviors with loose and tangential thoughts moving too quickly to catch. Speaking of these states, Eugene Bleuler (1963) said that we react to these experiences as something that threatens our very existence. Harry Stack Sullivan (1974) noted that the normal have an aversion for the insane. How can we learn to stomach states like this long enough to work with them? An idea from Jung helps us with the dilemma: "[T]he establishment of order and the dissolution of what has been established are at bottom beyond human control. The secret is that only that which can destroy itself is truly alive" (Jung, 1968, pp. 73–74).

John Perry realized this when he said that it is the order (the premorbid personality) that becomes the problem. The psychosis itself is the attempt by the psyche to destroy itself (the *putrefactio*) so that it can be reestablished in a new and revitalized form. He demonstrated this wonderfully in his book *The Far Side of Madness*.

Cross-culturally, this same pattern appears in Mircea Eliade's writings on shamanism and in anthropologist Victor Turner's (1987) research showing that various tribes actually sought this dissolved state for long periods of time as a key to initiation rites. Scholars call this state the *limen*, which means being in between doorways, or not yet one place or the other. In some traditional cultures young boys and girls stayed in this state as long as one year, as a transition from childhood to adulthood. Turner delineated three stages of the process: separation or dissolution, liminality, aggregation. He found that in times of sociocultural transition the limen phase was induced in the tribal initiates by tribal leaders as a rite of passage.

The limen consists of an area symbolic of no past and no future, yet both. The candidates are stripped of all clothing, have no place to live except the wilderness, and are nameless. Every trace of graspable identity is removed. Turner found that "logically antithetical processes" symbolize this period. For instance, the snake is chosen because it sheds and regrows its skin, the moon for its waxing and waning. The tunnel represents both the tomb and the womb. All symbolize the death and rebirth theme that occurs over and over again in work with extreme-state patients.

8. WHAT'S LOVE GOT TO DO WITH IT?

Everything! As therapists know, the ability to perform technical interventions does not equal cures, especially in psychotherapeutic work.
Interventions can help in the moment, often allowing the therapist to
get crucial information about split-off personality parts. But no technique will replace the feeling qualities of love, patience, and devotion.
"The thing that really matters is the personal commitment," Jung said,
noting that he had seen miraculous cures "as when sympathetic
nurses and laymen were able, by their courage and steady devotion, to
reestablish psychic rapport with their patients" (Jung, 1960, p. 265).

This idea was hammered home in the 1973 study of cross-cultural
psychosis by the World Health Organization. They found that in nonwesternized, nontechnical countries the cure rate and lack of recidivism far surpassed westernized, technologically developed countries
even with so-called modern treatment. The conclusion drawn was
that the nonwesternized countries keep individuals involved in the
community and therefore not isolated and ostracized (Sartorius,
Jablensky, & Shapiro, 1978).

NIHILO TAMEN INITIUM: ENDING YET BEGINNING

This paper was written 23 years ago for a conference on working
psychologically with extreme states of consciousness. I have rewritten
parts of it for this book, but in general the paper remains close to my
original musings. Yet I consider it fascinating that this many years
later the ideas endure in their topicality.

How could it be that so much of what is laid out in this work is
still not agreed upon or considered generally accepted knowledge in
the field? As I express in more detail in the chapter "Animal Eyes," we
have been lulled to sleep by the biochemical model. Jung says that "as
soon as [any model] is assumed to be generally valid," it "leads to absolute sterility" (of thought and research) (Jung, 1960, p. 155). There is
a dearth of funded research that offers exploration of psychotherapy

for psychoses, though the investigations out of Finland involving the Need-Adapted Model, and the immensely successful Open Dialogue programs, along with NIMH's RAISE studies in the United States, are at least beginning to move the pendulum. This new wave of psychosocial treatments is encouraging, especially with the advent of the Hearing Voices Movement and the excitement and worldwide growth of The International Society for Psychological and Social Approaches to Psychosis.

However, despite these very important and necessary moves away from the devastating beliefs of the "age of the brain" era of the 1990s, led by the bias of the Van Putten and P. R. A. May (1976) studies that denigrated milieu therapy for schizophrenia, it still does not go far enough in recognizing psychosis as the attempt by the psyche to heal itself. The most important message I take from Al de Half is the crucial realization that his world is a "separate reality" and requires a radical change of imagination if we are to truly understand the patients that have entered this foreign land with him. Until psychiatric hospitals and their treatment units move back in time toward therapeutic milieus, longer stays, less medication, and validating the environment as affecting the outcome of the process; until psychiatrists receive training in metaphor and symbol, finalistic causality, and the capability of the psyche to destroy itself to bring forth something new and possibly better, then psychiatrists will stay enamored by quick medication interventions. We will continue glueing the pieces of Humpty-Dumpty back together again, into his old self, rather than realizing that the psyche was attempting all along to reimagine itself into a higher and truer self.

JULIA AND THE LITTLE SHOOTS

THE MEMORY OF placing the small, oddly shaped piece of driftwood, weathered and beaten, rounded and grizzled, on the floor of my office brings a smile to my face. Julia's sessions often start like this. I come down to the waiting room to say hello, and usually she has just finished getting a beverage. I warm my ever-present mug of tea, and we go upstairs together. As we reach my office, I move this 35-year-old log that I found washed up on the shores of Lake Michigan during the years of my residency for Julia to place her cup on, while she, in turn, reaches down to pet my dog, Riley.

What is it about this ritual that gives me such pleasure? Is it a rite of entry to the doorway of the psyche? Jung smoked his pipe; Hillman took off his shoes; Riklin closed his eyes. I give my dog a treat, pull my Judd Hirsch–like sweater over my neck (think the great psychiatrist from the movie *Ordinary People*), and take hold of my hot cup of tea. I am now ready for psyche's stories to emerge.

The look in Julia's eyes on this day was edgy, and I could sense that something wasn't quite right. I had been seeing her for about six months, after a colleague referred her to me. Paranoid schizophrenia had been diagnosed previously, but she came to me hoping that with supportive psychotherapy, she could live a more normal life in the community. Unbeknownst to me, however, she had stopped taking her psychiatric medications.

My sense that something was off quickly became apparent, for just as I sat down in my rocking chair, she abruptly stood up, a look of both sadness and malice coming across her face as she shouted, "You don't water your plants! You should be ashamed." Walking over to my jade plant and standing beside it, she continued to lecture me. "They are just little shoots, tiny shoots that need water and sun."

Initially caught off guard but quickly adjusting my awareness to the emerging scene, I walked over to join her by the jade plant. I realized that no "observing ego" was available, and for the first time Julia became my teacher in what Jungian analyst Arnold Mindell was to call the "up periscope" technique (Mindell, personal communication). The idea is that if the ego observer or "fair witness" is underwater or swamped by the unconscious, the therapist must go underwater with the patient to have any success. This territory is lit by the moon. It is the realm of lunacy, soft light, and metaphor. In this realm the use by the therapist of sunlit logic or Herculean swordlike rationalism does not work and in fact exacerbates the problem. However, it is also incumbent upon the therapist to put up a "periscope" to hold the conscious, metaphorical position.

"Julia, you are so good with plants," I responded. "Thank you for helping me. I need your assistance to show me exactly how to take better care of this plant." I put out my arm and said, "My arm is like one of those shoots; please show me in detail what you would do." Right away, she gently touched my arm, and said softly, "Little shoots need love and tenderness and protection. People think they don't need attention. They just expect that the little shoots will grow and get big and strong without the special care they need."

I reached over and touched her arm saying, "Just like your parents didn't always care for your little shoots." Julia looked at me and began to tear up.

"My father always expected so much. He would never even hug me. I was expected to be perfect," she intoned, clearly now back on dry ground.

The session went on more typically, talking about her family life and why she was choosing not to take medication. We were able to avoid hospitalization on that day. Julia had many more psychotic moments and more hospitalizations, but for that brief session, the metaphorical bridge from the underworld to the day world held.

There are probably many metapsychological explanations for what happened with Julia. My way of understanding this clinical encounter is fairly simple. I entered the dream world that Julia was living in. I was able to do this congruently by believing in what Jung called "psychic reality." This is the world of fantasy, one that every therapist must take seriously. Jung was very clear about this point in his *Red Book* when he said, "[E]very unknown wanderer who personally inhabits the inner world...[is] real because they are effectual" (Jung, 2009, p. 260). He realized that the superstitious phobia that science had developed about fantasy would not protect us. "The real is what works" (Jung, 1966, p. 217).

Because of this belief I didn't need to make appeasing statements to Julia such as "I know that is your experience," or "I understand that is what you feel." These are messages that well-meaning parents might give their children (e.g., "Yes, honey, I know you think there are monsters under the bed, but there really aren't any. You're just dreaming."). Instead, I entered the dream reality and listened attentively to what Julia said, while holding the mythic, symbolic position described by Mindell. At that moment, it was reality! The patient's psychic truth was alive in the room and in the world. It was obvious that Julia was the "little shoots" and I, the "bad caretaker." This paradigm shift made it possible to experience the imaginal world, physically and symbolically, while still talking the patient's language.

The "up periscope" method allows a crossover to be built from one world to the other. If I can get the patient to show me exactly what they are referring to in a more relational manner, then often the figures come closer to living in a field between us and, with luck, connect us together to a shared reality in the day world.

Julia taught me all this on that memorable day: a session I have never forgotten, even with all the memories accumulated during the 35 years that old log and I had spent listening to psyche's musings.

THE BEARDED MAN

I WAS SITTING at my desk, just finishing the last of my therapy notes, when his plaintive request popped up. "Tom, please call me," the text read. "I need a consultation immediately. I think I may be psychotic or at least my world is turning upside down and crazy," ending with "your old medical school buddy, Jack Duncan." Surprised to hear from him, especially in this way, I hadn't seen Jack in years, not since he had moved his family from Milwaukee, accepting a teaching position with the neurology department at the University of Washington Medical School. We spoke every so often by phone, always promising to get together to catch up, but with our busy practices and family life our schedules never seemed to mesh. We had met in our residencies as we shared rotations throughout our four years. A close-knit group of friends had developed during that stressful time of training, with interns in psychology and residents from many disciplines all coming together to unwind on weekends, with ample servings of beer and long dance sessions led by Donna Summer and Thelma Houston. I dialed the number he left; he answered immediately.

"Tom, I need to see you tomorrow! I'll cancel my patients and drive down first thing. Everything is weird. My vacation home is haunted: pots banging, doorbells ringing, and my grandson drawing pictures of this man that I treated, a John Doe, that came out of coma briefly before dying. His pictures look just like him, especially the foot-long black beard that grew during his vegetative state. How can that be happening? I remembered you were always into that far-out stuff. What was it called? Jungian? I always made fun of you about it. Anyway, nobody up here is on the fringes like you are; it's pretty straitlaced at the school. I can't talk with anyone at my clinic or they will want to shoot me up with Thorazine. You've got to see me right away." I began asking him a few standard questions about voices, sleep, and levels of energy, but before I could finish he interrupted.

"Tom, I'm not manic or depressed or having any of Bleuler's A's, if that's what you are trying to find out. I'm sleeping great and until this started happening, my life couldn't have been going better, but now I don't understand. You know me, I'm a meat-and-potatoes guy. Give me a case of good old-fashioned multiple sclerosis, and I'm all over it, but I can't deal with all this psychic woo-woo shit. I feel like I'm in that Bruce Willis 'Six Senses' movie."

"That would be *The Sixth Sense*," I said laughing. Jack was able to laugh along with me, and I knew with his humor intact, all would be just fine. "This sounds like poltergeist phenomenon to me," I said, "and I have seen it in my practice in the past."

"Poltergeist?" he shouted excitedly. "I don't know what that is, I never saw that movie, but I'm thrilled you might have an idea. I knew you would. When can I come?"

"I'll see you at 7 a.m. at my office in Vancouver," I said. I gave him the address and told him to get some sleep and drive safe.

I was just turning on the lights and grabbing my first cup of tea when the door to my office building swung open. "Dr. Harper, you are a sight for sore eyes!" Jack said happily as he strode through the door, embracing me in his famous but long-forgotten bear hug. He still looked like a modern version of Grizzly Adams, a hulking man of six feet four inches and easily 240 pounds, with a bushy full beard, now gray-flecked, in keeping with his 62 years. I had agreed to see him first thing this morning, squeezing him in an hour earlier than the usual start to my day. He had left Seattle at 4 a.m. to make our appointment on time.

"Let me get you a cup of tea and we can head upstairs to my office," I offered.

"Are you kidding? I am not that genteel," Jack replied, a big smile crossing his face. "I just finished two of those Starbucks Iced Coffee Trentas, so I'm a little wired and also needing to find the head before we get started."

I showed him where the bathroom was and pointed the way to my office. I then took my customary seat in my favorite rocker and wondered about this strange psychic activation. How could a man Jack had treated for such a short time, never able to learn his story or even his real name, now enter his grandson's unconscious so precisely? Certainly this was very similar to what had happened to Jung and his children shortly before he wrote *Septem Sermones ad Mortuos*. Chuckling to myself, I thought, "Jack is not being called to write a great religious tome, but there may be an aspect of his unconscious he has been avoiding and is now coming out in the more accessible psyches of his grandchildren." I had seen this same phenomenon in my own practice when a woman came to see me for chronic anxiety and self-esteem issues. She clearly had repressed much of the feeling aspect of her life, especially in regard to her marriage. I asked for dreams, but she had none of her own. However, she told me about her nine-year-old son, who had begun acting out her specific psychic conflicts after he started having dreams of her long dead great-grandmother, who would visit him almost nightly, giving him information that was impossible for him to know otherwise. But just as I began to reflect further on how this could be occurring with Jack and his family, he had finished in the bathroom and was settling into the seat opposite me in the rocking chair.

"Tom, let's get right to it. You can be sure I would love to catch up on Elaine and the kids, and you would love to know about Staci and ours, but I've only got an hour with you and there is a lot to tell. Okay with you if we skip the pleasantries," Jack asked. I nodded yes.

"It all started about a month ago when I was on call during the week for our neurology group. I got a page from Harborview that there was a John Doe case, brought in by the police after finding him unconscious in an abandoned house off Feder Street in South Seattle. Apparently some kids were playing in the area and saw him lying on a mattress on the floor. No telling how long he had been there, but his beard had grown all the way down to his navel. We began calling him Rip at the hospital."

"You mean for Rip Van Winkle?" I asked, smiling.

"Yeah, you remember the gallows humor that happens with hospital staff from working with all the tragedy we see," Jack replied with a grin, but a slight catch in his voice and a fleeting look in his eyes betrayed the witnessing of years of life's sadder truths. He sat back on the couch, closing his eyes for just a moment, seemingly caught in the emotions that had arisen. Memories of "good old Jack Duncan" came flooding back to me. He was the life of every party: extroverted, beer in hand, loud and fun loving, and always absolutely sure about everything. He had a rapier wit and loved using it, making fun of all beliefs that lay outside his "only if you can touch it" test of reality. Any talk of dreams or the irrational brought on lectures about being unscientific and could open you up to his greatest scorn. But in the end Jack loved people and wanted as much as any of us back then to be a great doctor and to relieve suffering. But he was sure that meant only classic Western medicine and its theories. Nothing else was scientific. My awareness came abruptly back to the present as I saw him have a slight shake of his head as if to throw off these disturbing images before continuing.

"Anyway," he started up, "Rip stayed in that vegetative state for weeks, just lying there on his back. We labeled the cause idiopathic since we could never figure out what induced the coma. His electrolytes were a little off when he was first admitted, but they got straightened out pretty quick with the intravenous drips. All his other blood work and tests were normal, even his MRI. We put in a PICC line to feed him and did everything we could to keep him comfortable. The nurses even began brushing his hair and beard every day and laying it outside the sheets like he was Kris Kringle from the old movie *Miracle on 34th Street.*"

"It sounds like he brought out a lot of deep feelings in the ICU staff, and maybe you also?"

"There was something about him," Jack said, nodding. "I can't tell you what, just a sense when you came near his bed, an energy, a feeling, stuff I usually don't pay any mind to. Tom, I'm a corn-fed boy from Nebraska, and I don't typically chew on this kind of data. I'm a rational, logical neurologist, for God's sake, but Rip got to me. I started going out of my way to see him two or three times a day. First thing in the morning, last thing at night, I would just sit there by his bed and talk to him. 'Who are you? Where are you from? Isn't there any family you want us to call?' One day I had this overwhelming urge to touch his beard. Not sure why, but I reached and touched it and began to caress it, and then suddenly my hand hit something just underneath, near his throat. I pulled his beard away and there hanging around his neck was the most beautiful necklace with a silver feather pendant. I was shocked. We would never allow jewelry to stay on a patient, especially with the risk of possible infection when putting in a feeding line. I called the staff together, but no one could explain how this could have occurred, and everyone denied that they had anything to do with it.

"Now things get really interesting," Jack continued. "I took the necklace off him, but since it seemed like it was important somehow, maybe even religious, I decided to leave it on the nightstand next to him instead of putting it in storage lockup as hospital protocol required. I returned that evening, late, just before heading home. I knew it was irrational, but something kept pulling me to go. When I got there he was lying on his back as usual, when all at once he opened his eyes. They were the most amazing eyes: deep, reflective, drawing you down and in. I wanted to call a nurse to come over, but I found myself without voice and unable to move. I was in complete shock since after all these weeks I never expected him to recover. Suddenly his left hand was taking my hand in his, and then with his closed other hand, now clearly holding something in it, he reached out and placed his necklace in mine, gently closing my fingers over it. For what seemed like minutes he held my hand in both of his, all the while inspecting me with the most intense gaze, as if he were judging my readiness for his message. It was then he spoke to me.

"'The necklace has a proper owner; you will know him by his spirit and his dreams. Please promise me you will follow this task, it is crucial!' Instantly, without thinking, I nodded my head, agreeing to his apparent last request. He squeezed my hand, like he was saying goodbye, then shut his eyes and was gone! The alarms went off as his heart monitor flatlined. The nurses were there in a second with the crash cart, but I knew it was hopeless. It was like he had chosen that moment to go, and our technological prowess was not going to bring him back."

"Jack, that is one hell of a story," I said, amazed. "What did you end up doing with the necklace?"

"I keep in my pocket for whenever I find the right person to give it to," Jack answered quite seriously.

"So you're taking what Rip said as a task, a calling or religious devotion? I've never known you like that," I said, indicating my surprise.

"I've never felt anything like what I experienced with him. But Staci thought I had lost my mind, like Richard Dreyfuss when he kept trying to build that mountain out of dirt in *Close Encounters of the Third Kind*."

"Well, at least you're now getting the names of the movie references right," I said, laughing.

Jack smiled back, but a furrowed brow and more serious tone followed quickly as he replied, "I thought she was probably right and I wanted to get back to my normal life. I had become quite possessed, thinking constantly about Rip and the necklace and who was the right person to give it to. So I decided to go up to our vacation cabin and put it in storage there, getting it away from my everyday sight."

"I can guess what happened next," I said.

"Well, if you're guessing that is when the haunting started, you would be right," he replied. "At first, everything seemed fine and I was just going to work, playing with the grandkids, and spending my usual time with Staci. But then the dreams started happening. Weird dreams, and you know I have never put any stock in them. 'No scientific basis,' the old me would have said, but after my experience with Rip, some part of me was now open to thinking and wondering about them."

"Tell me one if you would," I requested.

"Okay," Jack said. "Here is the one that got it started: *I am leaving for work in the dream, like I usually do but somehow as I am walking to my car the atmosphere changes and becomes dark and ominous. I have a sense that the world is alive with every animal of the night peering at me through the bushes and trees, whispering, wondering about me, like they are objective observers, judging me, and all considering what I will do next in the drama. Suddenly I can hear something or someone coming up behind me and I immediately start running but my legs are like concrete and whatever was behind me is about to catch me.* I awake, sweating and panicky."

"An important dream. What did you do with it?" I asked.

"I didn't do anything, except not just say it was inconsequential. I don't know anything about interpreting dreams. They didn't cover that in my neurology residency," Jack said, laughing.

"Well, you're not alone, Jack. They are not covering dreams in psychiatry training either. But that's a whole other discussion. What if we were to look at this dream for a minute, would that be okay?"

"I would love to," he responded, nodding his head.

"One way to work with dreams is to not automatically ask 'what does this mean?' but instead stay close to the images and linger with them, like poetry. Allow them to speak with you or to you. If you must ask questions, instead of 'why and what,' ask 'who and how.' For instance, in this dream there is a change occurring; the everyday, routine, mundane world of work drivenness, the driving off with no awareness of the magic that surrounds you, is changing. Instead, the world is now alive, uncanny, dark, and irrational."

"Yeah, I feel different since my encounters with Rip; nothing seems the same and certainly everything seems more alive, including the pots and pans!"

I smiled at his haunting reference and continued, "You're in a life drama. Nature itself seems to be wondering what you will do at this crossroads, and it can see what is coming up from behind you, from your back and unknown side, before you can. At first you choose to run. My first analyst used to say to me, 'Are you running because something is chasing you, or are they chasing you because you're running?'"

"I never thought of it that way, but again I haven't really given any credence to dreams."

"But you see the old defenses, which had been effective ones and worked for a long time, will not work anymore, and now those young legs from your football days are as if in concrete. No more sprinting away from the unconscious other," I reflected back to him.

"Wow," Jack said, shaking his head. "That is all right there in those images? Amazing! There is a lot everyday medicine could do with dreams."

"I couldn't agree with you more. But let's not leave this one yet. The 'dream maker' says in the how question that it's only when you try to go off in your mundane, everyday, driven life of work that then something or someone comes up behind you. Who could be coming up behind you?"

"I'm not sure, Tom, but let me get your point straight. You're saying if dreams do mean something, it's within a context of specifics, when and then. So here when the unknown something is coming up behind me, then I am in my driving-off-to-work mentality?"

"Yes, that's exactly it," I said, nodding enthusiastically. "Images are very specific in dreams and the when and then give you the connection. When you're being approached by the other, then it is connected to your driving off, staying unconscious to a different way of being in the world and life. Something is changing or wants to change in you, Jack. What happened after this dream?"

"It affected me quite a bit. I had trouble focusing that day at work, so I told my wife I was going to take the afternoon off and try to go relax and collect my thoughts at the cabin. She was already planning on coming the next day with the grandkids, so she was fine with me going a day early. So I drove up, but everything seemed eerie and ominous, like something was about to happen. That night I had this dream: *I was at my vacation house when Rip appeared at my door, trying to break in, or at least that's what I thought. He looked younger but had the same long black beard. I ran to the door to try to lock it, but it was a brand-new door and was not yet stained and had no bolt lock or door knob installed yet. I heard him say quite sternly, 'Leave the door open!'* I awoke with the feeling that he would become more forceful if I did not obey this order."

"So now we know who was coming up behind you," I said. "Often 'dream series' give answers about previous dreams. Jung was of the opinion that sometimes one could never really interpret a dream until the dream series was known. We can see now that Rip is quite serious, and not interested in your ignoring him any longer."

"That's when I began to get more frightened. Was Rip a ghost stalking me? I didn't believe in ghosts or at least hadn't up until then, but given what occurred shortly after my wife and grandkids got to the vacation home, I've changed my mind."

"What happened at the house?" I asked, now on the edge of my seat, like I had been drawn into an exciting mystery novel.

"Well, I'll start with everyone arriving. My daughter has two kids, as you remember: Jennifer, who just turned 12, and Adam, who was six last month. We had them for the week while their parents went back East to visit my son-in-law's ailing mother. They arrived with Staci, and we had a nice afternoon looking for edible mushrooms and playing the deer-spotting game we've played for years while we walked to the lake to swim. When we got back I started to prepare dinner, getting the burgers and corn ready for grilling. Both grandkids were there helping me when suddenly the doorbell started ringing. But when we went to answer it, no one was there except the feel of a cool, chilling breeze that came blowing in through the open door, even though it was mid-July and 90 degrees outside. We all laughed, though I was admittedly a little spooked and became even more so when a thunderous sound came from the kitchen as pots began dropping off the pot rack over the stove. At the same time all the lights in the house began to flicker on and off. This went on for hours, with the grandkids asking, 'Grandpa, is the cabin haunted?'"

"When did it finally stop?" I asked.

"Adam had gone back to my office, which also acts as a spare bedroom when we have guests. He had taken Roscoe, our golden retriever, saying it was because Roscoe needed some exercise, but we all knew it was for protection. Suddenly I heard the dog growl and Adam screaming, 'Grandpa, grandma, Jennifer, come here!' We ran back to them, but no one was there except him and Roscoe. He told us he was sure he had seen someone in the room trying to get into the filing cabinet. It was in that cabinet I had locked the silver necklace weeks before. I asked Adam what he had seen and he said he could draw him. Tom, I am telling you it was uncanny. Adam has some natural drawing talent like his grandmother, and he drew a spitting image of Rip from my dream. White T-shirt, dark blue jeans, work boots, and a deep black beard down to his belly button.

"I suddenly realized what I had to do and told everyone to leave, shutting the door behind them. I got the necklace out of the cabinet and then I spoke to him, like I was one of your schizophrenic patients. 'Rip, I have the necklace and I'll keep my promise and find the rightful owner. Please stop scaring everyone. I will follow through!' I heard nothing back, no verbal response, but suddenly, at almost that same moment, the curtain at the window rustled and I felt the same cool breeze on my cheek as earlier, though no window in the room was open. I have kept the necklace in my possession ever since, and no further hauntings or dreams have occurred. I called you the next day and you said you might know what was happening, something about a poltergeist?"

"Yes," I answered. "It means 'noisy ghost' in German. The types of things that were happening at your cabin are usually associated with it. Pictures coming off walls, loud banging, furniture moving. It seems to not be related to the place as much as being associated with a person who is being picked out, often because they have broken a promise to someone after they died. In this case you broke the promise. Also, when so-called hauntings or ghostly events occur, they are often associated with the same experiences of the cool breeze that you felt. 'In Greek *psychein* means "to exhale," *psychros* "cold," and *psychos* "cool." Thus psyche or soul may actually be defined as a "cool breath or breeze"''' (Jaffé, 1979, p. 128).

"Jesus, Tom, that's a pretty far-out explanation even for you. There has got to be another way of making sense rationally of what was taking place that day. Maybe minor earth temblors, or down drafts in the chimney. Come on now!" Jack had already dismissed the glaring fact that he had actually talked to Rip's "ghost."

"You're right, there was probably a down draft in the chimney that blew the pots down, while at the same time a minor earth temblor rattled the electrical system and set the lights flickering and the doorbell ringing," I said facetiously. "Of course this probably also created the 'cool draft' you felt in the heat of a summer day. However, none of these rationalizations can explain how Adam could draw Rip so accurately, does it? And it doesn't take into account that when you reacted like a person from ancient times, taking what was occurring seriously as if it were real and then emotionally responding to it, the haunting stopped immediately.

"Let me tell you a story from my greatest teacher, Carl Jung, to illustrate this," I said. I leaned back in my rocker and reaching back to the bookshelf behind me, got my copy of Jung's autobiography, *Memories, Dreams, Reflections*. "I want to read you this amazing account Jung tells about an experience he had with his neighbor shortly after the neighbor's death. The story begins with Jung in bed, saying:

> I lay awake thinking of the sudden death of a friend whose funeral had taken place the day before. I was deeply concerned. Suddenly I felt that he was in the room. It seemed to me that he stood at the foot of my bed and was asking me to go with him. I

did not have the feeling of an apparition; rather, it was an inner visual image of him, which I explained to myself as a fantasy. But in all honesty I had to ask myself, "Do I have any proof that this is a fantasy? Suppose it is not a fantasy, suppose my friend is really here and I decided he was only a fantasy—would that not be abominable of me?" Yet I had equally little proof that he stood before me as an apparition. Then I said to myself, "Proof is neither here nor there! Instead of explaining him away as a fantasy, I might just as well give him the benefit of the doubt and for experiment's sake credit him with reality." The moment I had that thought, he went to the door and beckoned me to follow him. So I was going to have to play along with him! That was something I hadn't bargained for. I had to repeat my argument to myself once more. Only then did I follow him in my imagination.

He led me out of the house, into the garden, out to the road, and finally to his house. (In reality it was several hundred yards away from mine.) I went in, and he conducted me into his study. He climbed on a stool and showed me the second of five books with red bindings which stood on the second shelf from the top. Then the vision broke off. I was not acquainted with his library and did not know what books he owned. Certainly I could never have made out from below the titles of the books he had pointed out to me on the second shelf from the top.

This experience seemed to me so curious that next morning I went to his widow and asked whether I could look up something in my friend's library. Sure enough, there was a stool standing under the bookcase I had seen in my vision, and even before I came closer I could see the five books with red bindings. I stepped up on the stool so as to be able to read the titles. They were translations of the novels of Emile Zola. The title of the second volume read: *The Legacy of the Dead* (Jung, 1973a, pp. 312–313).

"Wow, that's an incredible story," Jack said. "I think I see what you're getting at. That my making it either rational or crazy is not the best way to go."

"Yes!" I exclaimed. "What Jung is trying to teach us is that 'rationalism and doctrinairism are the disease of our time; they pretend to have all the answers' (Jung, 1973a, p. 300). In my opinion he is showing that many times we can't say what is absolutely real or not, but you can, as he did, treat it as if it is and give it your emotional attention. You did that with Rip, as Jung did with the vision of his neighbor, and the results are obvious."

"Okay, I get it. I just needed to hear your explanation, because it seemed so crazy to me. But I know that is what I actually experienced, and all the haunting did stop after that. Now what do I do? What's the next move?"

I looked at the clock and realized it was just a few minutes away from my eight o'clock patient. "We're going to have to stop, but what if you spent the weekend. Elaine would love to see you, and we could talk more about this. I have some other ideas from the material you told me that I would like to share."

"That sounds great," Jack said, clearly looking relieved that we would have more time together. "I'll give Staci a call and tell her the plans. She'll be happy we are figuring this out; she was pretty shook up. I'll go get some breakfast and wander around Portland, and then meet you at your house tonight. Tell Elaine I'll do the cooking tonight for my room and board. How about a couple of rib-eyes on the grill?"

"Love it," I said, laughing. "Get some of that Cherry Garcia ice cream we used to eat back when we were on call together. We'll pull an all-nighter, drink wine, eat ice cream, and talk ghosts."

"What could be more fun? It's a deal," Jack said, smiling, and with that he gave me another bear hug. "Thanks, Tom, I really appreciate this. I'm already feeling better. See you tonight."

Jack headed down the steps, and I stepped back into my office just a minute before beginning my regular therapy day. "Ghosts, cool breezes, and ringing doorbells with no one there," I thought to myself. "I'll bet this will qualify as the most unusual content I hear in my sessions today."

I grabbed the bowls, the ice cream, and our second bottle of wine, as Jack settled into the recliner, readying ourselves for a night of stories and scintillating discussion. Elaine had said goodnight, heading off to bed to get some sleep before her early morning photography shoot. We all had lingered at the dinner table, late into the evening, enjoying Jack's steaks and the memories of Milwaukee days. Now, with the wine poured and the ice cream dished out, Jack started our evening talk.

"Do you really believe in ghosts, Tom?"

"Hell of a way to start us out!" I said laughing. "It's hard not to with all that you told me today. But what I can say after doing therapy for 35 years is that I am open to the irrational and believe there are many things our rational mind cannot explain. I have seen lots of cases that are shocking and hard to comprehend with logical, linear, and classic scientific methods; or as Karl Popper might say, I would have trouble applying conjecture and refutation to some of the patients I have seen through the years. One example is the story of a 22-year-old man who had a dream of *building an ark like Noah's, but he was on an island where the ocean was rising faster and faster and engulfing the land. The problem was he was building the boat out of bamboo and mud and it was clearly going to leak.* He had a psychotic break two weeks later. How could his psyche have known that ahead of time?"

"That's bizarre," Jack responded. He hesitated for a moment, then said, "I have been reticent to share any stories like this, and actually you will be the first person I've told that I have seen and heard cases like this over the years in my practice also; but I always tried to ignore them, worrying that my colleagues would think I was nuts if I mentioned it. I once saw a case of a 48-year-old woman who came to see me for chronic headaches that her primary care doctor had been treating as atypical migraines. She had a normal neurological exam with no lateralizing signs and was feeling somewhat better on the medication he had started her on. I was thinking we could just watch her for a while to see if she continued to improve. But before setting up a follow-up appointment, I asked if there was anything else she thought I should know. She said she had the most unusual dream the previous night. She dreamt that *she was reading an old story by Loren Eiseley titled "The Star Thrower," but in the dream she was helping the man throw the starfish back into the ocean when suddenly one of the starfish came at her, landing on her head, where it stuck and she was unable pry it off.* She awoke panicked. I realized that one type of brain tumor is an astrocytoma, which arises from astrocytes. I don't know if you remember your brain anatomy, Tom, but astrocytes are star-shaped, like starfish, and are part of the glial cells that make up the supportive tissue. I decided to order an MRI based on her dream and sure enough she had a very early, grade I, pilocytic astrocytoma. She had surgery and we saved her life. She sang my praises around the department, and I was asked to present the case at a grand rounds, but I couldn't get myself to tell anyone that I made my most crucial decision in her evaluation, not based on science, but on her dream."

"Jack, that is an amazing case story. You were like a reincarnation of old Asclepius himself and his dream temples."

"What do mean, dream temples, and who was Asclepius?"

"He was the Greek god of medicine and had his famous dream temples called Asclepeion on the island of Kos in the fifth century BC. You would go there and be placed in a hole with a *kilné* or bed to lie on; it is where the name for our medical clinic comes from today. You would stay there until you had a dream and then tell the dream priest and that would indicate what to do. It was at these same temples that Hippocrates, the father of medicine, was said to have learned the art."

"That's fascinating," Jack responded. "But you're telling me we have not followed up on what was known 2400 years ago about dreams and illness? How about Jung? Did he look into this connection between dreams and disease states?"

"Yes, in fact one of his famous students, C. A. Meier actually wrote a book on Asclepian dream incubation. Jung himself spent many of his later years theorizing about what he termed the 'psychoid unconscious' and the possible connection to matter and the body. He said that '[s]ince psyche and matter are contained in one and the same world, and moreover are in continuous contact with one another and ultimately rest on irrepresentable, transcendental factors, it is not only possible but fairly probable, even, that psyche and matter are two different aspects of one and the same thing'" (Jung, 1960, p. 215).

"Tom, that's too abstract for me," Jack said. "Give me some examples of what he means."

"Well, your dream case is a great example, but I will tell you a couple of other shocking illustrations. Once Dr. Jung was asked by another doctor to consult on a case from just the dream alone. The dream was this: *'Someone beside me kept on asking me something about oiling some machinery. Milk was suggested as the best lubricant. Apparently I thought that oozy slime was preferable. Then, a pond was drained, and amid the slime there were two extinct animals. One was a minute mastodon. I forgot what the other was.'* Jung, from this dream, diagnosed the damming-up of cerebrospinal fluid in the right ventricle. He apparently was absolutely correct, and the physician, Dr. Davie, was to have said in his published report that 'dreams...do not merely provide information on the psychological situation, but may disclose the presence of organic disorder and even denote its precise location' (Lockhart, 2012, p. 61). Jung never said how he came to the conclusions he did with the images of the dream, though if you wanted to read a very plausible discussion of the symbols and how he came to his conclusions, you could read Russell Lockhart's paper 'Cancer in Myth and Dream.' I think what might be said from your example and this one is that 'bodily organs and processes have the capacity to stimulate the production of psychic images, meaningfully related to the type of physical disturbance and its location' (Lockhart, 2012, p. 62).

"One of my favorite stories of the effects of repressed aspects of the psyche causing illness in a family is a case story by Edward Whitmont, M.D., a famous analyst from the New York Jung Institute. He tells of being consulted about a young girl, age seven, who was suffering from intractable asthma. She had been treated with conventional medicine by multiple specialists and was still, even while on medications, having difficulty controlling her symptoms. She had come from what appeared to be an excellent family, the father being a small-businessman and the mother a school teacher. The mother was well-read, a church goer, and a 'have everything planned and in its proper place' type of person. The young girl was very close to her mother and well adapted but possibly overcontrolled. Whitmont asked for dreams from both, and here is what was reported. The mother's recurrent dream was this: *'I am with a group of women, all masquerading as angels. A man is trying to break into the house, even though all the doors and windows are barred and shut tight. He is an Eastern potentate, and he says that if I do not let him in, he is going to kill the child.'* The child's recurrent dream was described in these words: *'I am trying to get onto an island from the water, but the "goat people" or sometimes a "huge great goat-man" will not let me on the land, but always pushes me back into the water.'*

"Jack, you can begin to understand without much dream training what Whitmont saw," I commented. "The mother was being too good and too one-sided, or as the dream says, 'masquerading as angelic.' This leaves a great power and energy outside of her psychic life and, as in one of my cases I had been thinking of earlier, causes the repressed figure to be embodied unconsciously and more negatively by the children in the household. This shows in the child's dream as the goat-man pushing her back in the water—in this case preventing any foothold on life and constricting her spirit and then manifesting as the somatic symbolism of asthma. Here the analyst was able to show through mythological amplification and symbolism, as did Jung in the dream we just talked about, that the Eastern potentate and the goat-man were one and the same figure. In this instance it was an aspect of the mother's deeper psyche that needed awareness and development, lest it turn its negative effects upon the daughter. Whitmont began to treat the mother and amazingly the child's asthma resolved" (Whitmont, 1979, pp. 43–46).

"Those are all remarkable stories," Jack said. "It makes me feel excited to possibly come out more at the medical school with some of my own experiences and thoughts in this direction. I was imagining, while you were telling me your tales, about running a dream group for the neurology residents, looking at the connection of psyche and soma.

I wish you could be there with me; I don't think I'm quite ready to lead dream seminars alone."

"I have an idea," I said. "I was thinking you might enjoy working with Bill McIntyre, my old analyst from the Chicago Jung Institute. He is still seeing a handful of patients and has a passion for the somatic aspect of the psyche."

"I would love that," Jack said, excited. "You would call him for me?"

"I'll call him tomorrow, right away. His office is close to the medical school, and I think with what is happening with you, he could be quite helpful." Jack nodded his thanks. But just as I started to tell one more case story, I saw him fighting off a yawn, his eyes barely capable of remaining open.

"Jack, I just looked at my watch. You've been up for almost 24 hours. I got so carried away with my stories, I wasn't paying attention to how exhausted you must be. Let's call it a night."

"I thought I could keep going, like old times, but I guess there are a few more years weighing us down," he said, chuckling. "I'll see you in the morning and tell you any dreams I have tonight."

"That's a deal," I said as we stood and headed off for bed.

The early morning summer light was playing hide and seek with the clouds, scurrying in and out of our east-facing bedroom window. Elaine was already up and gone for work, and I could hear Jack in the kitchen, fumbling with the coffee pot, making a valiant effort to obtain some much-needed caffeine. I stretched my aging back, rolled out of bed, and after grabbing my robe, headed to Jack's Keurig rescue.

"Hell, Tom, what kind of contraption is this?" Jack said, clearly frustrated.

"Well, good morning to you too, Jack!" I said, laughing. "We have that coffee maker to test our guests' IQs. If you can figure it out on your first try, we give it to you as a prize."

"I need the caffeine to get my neurons firing, so I may be the lucky one in this case. Hey, any dreams pop up for you last night? 'Cause I sure had a couple of whip-dousers."

"I slept the sleep of the dead, so didn't have any I can remember. But tell me yours as I grab some tea," I responded.

"I had the damnedest dream about Roger Federer. You know I'm a big tennis fan and still play some myself. Anyway, in the dream *he had badly injured his knee and could no longer play and had to retire. He was so devastated by this that he committed suicide.* I awoke, sad and grieving."

"A big dream, Jack. A whole way and attitude of life is ending," I replied. "What was your next dream? They are always connected."

"I went back to sleep and woke up after dreaming *about Rip's necklace. It was as if hanging in space, the silver feather pendant very prominent in its display.*"

"How incredible!" I said, shaking my head with amazement. "As long as I live I will never get over how dreams can say things in a way our everyday consciousness could never put together."

"Tell me what you're seeing and realizing," Jack eagerly requested.

"Well, it is fascinating that your dream picked Federer to amplify its point. Tell me quickly what you associate to him. A pop-up association. I say "Federer" and you say...?"

"Hero, the best ever!"

"Now keep going with what comes to mind," I added.

"The GOAT, 'greatest of all time.' Graceful, flowing, like moving above the ground as he ran," Jack continued.

"That's what is changing, and being sacrificed: the hero and its ego attachment to that energy. But here is the amazing part from the dream maker. You told me yesterday that Rip was found unconscious on Feder Street in Seattle."

"Jesus, Tom, that's unbelievable. What could that mean?" Jack said with a look of surprise.

"First let's talk about what one of my great teachers showed me through the years. He discovered that 'words are eggs' (Lockhart, 2012), that in their etymology they contained the unconscious history of the word and often reopen and allow us to 're-spect' their insights anew. The name *Federer* comes from *feder*, which means 'feather' in German. It's also connected to the old English *fiderian*, meaning to 'furnish with feathers or wings,' which relates to 'fitting an arrow with feathers' and 'feathering one's nest' or 'enriching oneself.' It's also associated with the root *ptero*, meaning 'feather' or 'wing,' and the root *pet*, meaning 'to rush; fly.' Lastly, it's associated in Slavonic with *pero*, 'pen.'

"So if we put this all together it says something like this: That the time of 'feathering your own nest' and enriching your ego—that time in life of the hero and 'your arrow flying high and straight,' feathered with all its accomplishments—is coming to an end. Instead, that energy is transforming or wanting to transform to something 'other.' It is now a silver feather, silver being associated typically with the feminine and with the imagination. The feather is also the spiritual world, a call to a relationship with something greater than the 'I.' It's the unconscious asking you 'to keep the door open,' to be open to a relationship to the 'other' and its voice."

"I don't understand yet," Jack said, a worried look on his face. "Am I dying, going to the spirit world as you're saying?"

"Only metaphorically, Jack, only metaphorically! You have always been quite successful. You were a big sports star and then a staff doctor at a famous medical school. But these things wear out and often something more is asked that is not of your ego's making; a connection is being offered to something else, something more. Rip said the necklace has a proper owner and you will re-cognize him, know him once again, by his spirit and his dreams. Jack, it is this 'you' that Rip wants you to recognize. It is your necklace, and your new life. It's beginning to show in your wanting to come out with long-repressed ideas, start a dream group for residents, work with Bill McIntyre, and who knows what else?" We both sat quietly for what seemed minutes and I was sure I saw a tear in his eye just before he spoke.

"Tom, that was very powerful and moving. I'm overwhelmed with what has been occurring in the last month and all that my dreams are now saying. I said earlier to you that I thought I was going crazy, but now I think or feel that something more meaningful may be trying to happen. I'm going to take you up on sessions with your old analyst, and I'll see where life points from there. As for the necklace, somehow, without knowing all that you did about the dreams, I came to the same conclusion." He pulled back his shirt collar and there sat the pendant, hanging beautifully around his neck, looking like it had been handcrafted just for him.

"Let's get something to eat," I said. "We've done more important dream work before breakfast than I usually do in a whole day of seeing patients." The morning went by pleasantly, as we ate and cleaned up. While Jack got packed and ready to get on the road home, I gave Bill McIntyre a call. He couldn't have been more pleased about seeing my friend and thought he could get him in this week, telling me to have Jack call him later today after his drive.

"Tom, I can't thank you enough for all you have done. I promise to keep in touch and let you know how things are going. Also, be prepared, I'm going to get you and Elaine to come up to visit and have you as a guest lecturer at my new dream group."

"I can't wait," I said, and we hugged one last time, the embrace carrying a little more heartfelt squeeze from us both.

 A couple of weeks passed before Jack called. He had connected with Dr. McIntyre, and they hit it off right away. He felt analysis was going to be very meaningful and was already making changes in his life direction. One of these, he told me, was that the medical school had approved his proposal of a dream group for neurology residents and fellows, and in fact asked if he might consider doing some research in the area of dreams and psychosomatic issues. Apparently the son of the dean of students had been suicidal during his adolescence and had gone to see Bill for therapy. The dean felt Dr. McIntyre had saved his son's life and was now a convert to all things Jungian. Who could have known?

I went to bed that night, thinking about Jack and the couple of days we spent together, talking about Rip, his dreams, and the unusual psychic push he had gotten to change his life direction. I reflected for a moment about my own life and its current course. Was it getting a little stale? Was I envious of Jack and his powerful call from the psyche? I smiled, hoping that I had been trained well enough to follow my body signals and dream hints so that ghostly phenomenon wouldn't need to be my impetus for change. I leaned over and kissed Elaine goodnight and turned out my reading light by the bed.

"Tom, wake up," Elaine was whispering, while shaking my shoulder to wake me. "Did you hear that? I think the front door just came open." Slowly coming out of sleep and having a vague sense of having been in a dream, I got up from the bed, telling her I would check on it. I couldn't believe anyone had broken in and was sure I had locked the door before coming up to bed. Elaine sat ready to call 911 if needed.

I went to the top of the steps and turned on the lights and all looked fine. Going down slowly, I could see that the front door was wide open, but with no one around. I turned a light on in the living room and also the kitchen, but everything was in place and untouched. I went to the front door and looked outside, but there was no sign of anyone. I looked at the door and lock and nothing showed signs of being jimmied. Then suddenly I thought of Jack's dream of Rip and being told to "leave the door open." "No, that couldn't be it, could it?" I said to myself. Then the dream came back, the one I was in when Elaine was shaking me awake. *The door to our house was wide open and sitting on the stoop was an antique school writing desk with an ink well. On it, next to the ink well, was a quill feather and, next to the feather, a book of stories by Washington Irving.*

As I started up the stairs to tell Elaine everything was okay, I smiled and looked to the heavens and said, "Rip, I promise you, I will start to write!"

CASTLE CALLINGS

THE FEATHER FROM the old pillow tickled my nose as the sun streamed in the living room window, leaving sheaths of light playing across thick 1970s wall-to-wall carpet. It was my sister's apartment in San Francisco, and I was just coming to consciousness on her sofa. As usual, when we sisters get together the wine flows freely, as my cotton mouth and pounding head were now attesting. This bout of debauchery was more than usual though. I had come for solace—my fourth relationship breakup in the last five years was fresh and painful. Between the glasses of red wine, the anger spewing, and the broken water main of tears, I told her about my embarrassing neediness and pleading dependency, all compressed in one final night with the "latest him."

I told her of the holding, grabbing, reaching out in aching longing, as he drove away in disgust. I also told her of that same dream, the one that had been happening for years. *The reaching hands for my neck, the sense of being pulled into oblivion.* We had talked about this before and thought it was related to my wounds from a mother clinging to both of us in ways that prevented escape and our own independent lives. I seemed the more wounded of the two of us, my sister slipping away into analysis, then becoming a therapist herself. I had tried therapy a couple of times, but never could trust all the psychobabble they threw around. I knew my sister wouldn't judge me, plus she had lived in that same crazy home. She knew!

I remembered now, as my brain started to clear with my first cup of coffee, that the dream seemed a little different from before. *The castle was more prominent this time and the man beckoning me to come in from the second floor window, more compelling.* I was usually angry after the dream that I had been duped and had fallen again for stupid childish desires. I couldn't let myself imagine that anything could ever be different. But why when I was driving up from Los Angeles did weird things keep happening? I remembered my sister had called them synchro somethings. She said that meant a so-called coincidence related to my inner life. I told her I thought she had had too much Pinot and was lost in her psycho-lingo. But I couldn't explain what was going on by just sheer coincidence either.

I heard my sister finally stirring in the other room, clearly out of drinking practice and moving even more slowly than I was. "Hurry up," I hollered, "I'll get you some coffee, and then I need you to hear this wacky synchro-psyche-stuff."

She appeared, with a less than "I can't wait to hear this" look on her face and the incredulous response: "You mean 'synchronicity'?"

"Yes, that weird-meaning stuff," I quickly replied, ignoring her sarcasm and handing her a mug of strong black java. "I didn't tell you everything last night. As I was leaving for the trip I decided to check the mail. Among the letters was a brochure for a "once in a lifetime trip to the Land of Castles—Tour the United Kingdom."

"I remember," Sis shot back, "that was what I told you was the synchronous event."

"Yeah, but I didn't tell you the rest," I said excitedly. "I was driving about an hour later on the freeway, listening to some music, when a car pulled into my lane with the California license plate: Castle-1. I was stunned, especially after seeing the brochure. I kept driving, thinking this was quite a coincidence, and decided to pull off for something to eat. I see my favorite hamburger joint, In-N-Out Burger, and pull in next to a panel truck. I look up and gasp! On the side it says Castle Interior Decorating.

"What do you think this means? Am I supposed to do anything, or am I just being silly, a new age woo-woo?" I said with a clear note of confusion in my voice. My sister sat quietly, not saying anything for the longest time, seeming in reverie.

Suddenly, she got up, saying, "Oh my God." She walked straight to her purse, fumbled around for a second, and pulled out a business card. "I was too drunk last night to remember this," she said with clear excitement. "We get these all the time, therapists are always moving to town and starting a practice, so it didn't come to mind."

"Well, what is the big deal then?" I asked. She handed me the card. We both looked at each other in amazement, incapable of speaking a word.

∽

The address was 1290 Fulton Avenue. I walked up the steps to the entrance, glancing quickly at what looked like a second-story office window. At the top of the steps was the professional signage:

JOHN CASTLE, M.D.
JUNGIAN ANALYST
WELCOME. PLEASE COME IN.

COPYRIGHT AND ATTRIBUTION ACKNOWLEDGMENTS

The author is grateful to the following organizations and publications that granted permission to reprint material contained in this book.

The C. G. Jung Institute of Los Angeles granted permission to reprint the story "Jung's Lament," which first appeared in *Psychological Perspectives* (2016), Vol. 59, Issue 3, pp. 376–390.

"On Life After Death" from MEMORIES, DREAMS, REFLECTIONS by C.G. Jung, translated by Richard and Clara Winston, edited by Aniela Jaffe, translation copyright © 1961, 1962, 1963 and renewed 1989, 1990, 1991 by Penguin Random House LLC. Used by permission of Pantheon Books, an imprint of the Knopf Doubleday Publishing Group, a division of Penguin Random House LLC. All rights reserved.

"Julia and the Little Shoots" was first published on the *Psychiatric Times* website on March 6, 2017. The essay won an "honorable mention" in the *Psychiatric Times* writer's contest, in which readers were invited to write about that one single patient who made them a better psychiatrist. www.psychiatrictimes.com/blogs/couch-crisis/julia-and-little-shoots

REFERENCES

Bertolote, J., & McGorry, P. (2005). Early intervention and recovery for young people with early psychosis: Consensus statement. *The British Journal of Psychiatry, 187*(48), s116–s119. doi: 10.1192/bjp.187.48.s116

Bleuler, M. (1963). Conceptions of schizophrenia within the last fifty years and today. *Proceedings of the Royal Society of Medicine, 56.*

Bola, J. R., & Mosher, L. R. (2003). Treatment of acute psychosis without neuroleptics: Two-year outcomes from the Soteria project. *The Journal of Nervous and Mental Disease, 191,* 219–229.

Bowen, E. (1975). *Pictures and conversations.* New York, NY: Alfred A. Knopf.

Burroway, J. (2007). *Imaginative writing: The elements of craft.* New York, NY: Penguin Academics.

Carpenter, W. (1977). The treatment of acute schizophrenia without drugs. *American Journal of Psychiatry, 134,* 14–20.

Castaneda, C. (1971). *A separate reality.* New York, NY: Simon and Schuster.

Eliade, M. (2004). *Shamanism: Archaic techniques of ecstasy.* Princeton, NJ: Princeton University Press.

Gorky, M. (1920). *Reminiscences of Leo Nikolaevich Tolstoy.* S. S. Koteliansky & L. Woolf, Trans. New York, NY: B. W. Huebsch, Inc.

Gottschall, J. (2012). *The storytelling animal: How stories make us human.* New York, NY: Houghton Mifflin Harcourt Publishing.

Halifax, J. (1988). *Shaman: The wounded healer.* London, England: Thames & Hudson.

Harrington, A. (2008). *The cure within: A history of mind-body medicine.* New York, NY: W. W. Norton and Company.

Harrington, A. (Ed.). (1997). *The placebo effect: An interdisciplinary exploration.* Cambridge, MA: Harvard University Press.

Harrow, M., Jobe, T. H., & Faull, R. N. (2012). Do all schizophrenia patients need antipsychotic treatment continuously throughout their lifetime? A 20-year longitudinal study. *Psychological Medicine, First View Articles,* 1–11. doi:10.1017/S0033291712000220

Hillman, J. (1975). *Re-visioning psychology.* New York, NY: Harper & Row.

Hillman, J. (1983). *Healing fiction.* Woodstock, CT: Spring Publications.

Hillman, J. (1985). *Anima: Anatomy of a personified notion.* Dallas, TX: Spring Publications.

Hillman, J. (1998). *Healing fiction.* Dallas, TX: Spring Publications.

Hillman, J., & Shamdasani, S. (2013). *Lament of the dead: Psychology after Jung's Red Book.* New York, NY: W. W. Norton and Company.

Humbert, E. (1984). *C. G. Jung: The fundamentals of theory and practice.* Wilmette, IL: Chiron Publications.

Jaffé, A. (1979). *Apparitions: An archetypal approach to death, dreams and ghosts.* Irving, TX: Spring Publications.

Jaffé, A. (1984). *Jung's last years.* Dallas, TX: Spring Publications.

Jung, C. G. (1960). *Collected works of C. G. Jung, volume 3: The psychogenesis of mental disease.* Princeton, NJ: Princeton University Press.

Jung, C. G. (1966). *Collected works of C. G. Jung, volume 7: Two essays on analytical psychology.* Princeton, NJ: Princeton University Press.

Jung, C. G. (1967). *Collected works of C. G. Jung, volume 13: Alchemical studies.* Princeton, NJ: Princeton University Press.

Jung, C. G. (1968). *Collected works of C. G. Jung, volume 12: Psychology and alchemy.* Princeton, NJ: Princeton University Press.

Jung, C. G. (1969). *Collected works of C. G. Jung, volume 8: The structure and dynamics of the psyche*. Princeton, NJ: Princeton University Press.

Jung, C. G. (1970). *Collected works of C. G. Jung, volume 14: Mysterium coniunctionis*. Princeton, NJ: Princeton University Press.

Jung, C. G. (1971). *Collected works of C. G. Jung, volume 6: Psychological types*. Princeton, NJ: Princeton University Press.

Jung, C. G. (1973a). *Memories, dreams, reflections*. A. Jaffé, Ed. New York, NY: Pantheon Books.

Jung, C. G. (1973b). *Collected works of C. G. Jung, volume 2: Experimental researches*. Princeton, NJ: Princeton University Press.

Jung, C. G. (1975). *Letters, Vol. 2: 1951–1961*. G. Adler & A. Jaffé, Eds. Princeton, NJ: Princeton University Press.

Jung, C. G. (1987). Introduction. In J. W. Perry, *The self in psychotic process*. Dallas, TX: Spring Publications.

Jung, C. G. (2009). *The red book*. S. Shamdasani, Ed. New York, NY: W. W. Norton and Company.

Jung, C. G. (2010). *Answer to Job*. Princeton, NJ: Princeton University Press.

Jung, C. G. (2015). *The psychology of dementia praecox* . Princeton, NJ: Princeton University Press.

Keeney, B. (2010). *The bushman way of tracking God*. New York, NY: Atria Books.

Laing, R. D. (1971). *The politics of experience*. New York, NY: Ballantine Books.

Lockhart, R. A. (2012). *Words as eggs: Psyche in language and clinic*. Everett, WA: The Lockhart Press.

Lown, B. (1996). *The lost art of healing: Practicing compassion in medicine*. Boston, MA: Houghton Mifflin Company.

Meier, C. A. (2009). *Healing dream and ritual: Ancient incubation and modern psychotherapy*. Einsiedeln, Switzerland: Daimon Verlag.

Menninger, K. (1963). *The vital balance: The life process in mental health and illness*. New York, NY: The Viking Press.

Merriam-Webster Dictionary. (2017). Medical definition of "DRG." Retrieved from https://www.merriam-webster.com/dictionary/DRG

Mindell, A. (1993). *The shaman's body: A new shamanism for transforming health, relationships, and the community.* San Francisco, CA: HarperSanFrancisco.

Mindell, A. (2000). *Dreaming while awake: Techniques for 24-hour lucid dreaming.* Charlottesville, VA: Hampton Roads Publishing Company.

Mindell, A. (2001). *Dreammaker's apprentice: Using heightened states of consciousness to interpret dreams.* Charlottesville, VA: Hampton Roads Publishing Company.

Mindell, A. (2013). *Dance of the ancient one: How the universe solves personal and world problems.* Portland, OR: Deep Democracy Exchange.

Mosher, L. R., Menn, A., & Matthews, S. M. (1975). Soteria: Evaluation of a home-based treatment for schizophrenia. *American Journal of Orthopsychiatry, 45*(3), 455–467. doi:10.1111/j.1939-0025.1975.tb02556.x

Novick, D. M., Swartz, H. A., & Frank, E. (2010). Suicide attempts in bipolar I and bipolar II disorder: A review and meta-analysis of the evidence. *Bipolar Disorders, 12*(1), 1–9. doi:10.1111/j.1399-5618.2009.00786.x

Olen Butler, R. (2001). *Inside creative writing.* Updated by Florida State University, 2014. Retrieved from https://www.youtube.com/watch?v=vIcnmiT0Mc8&index=1&list=PLTCv6n1whoI23GmdBZienRW0Q0nFCU_ay

Olen Butler, R., & Burroway, J. (2005). *From where you dream.* New York, NY: Grove Press.

Perceval, J. (1961). *Perceval's narrative: A patient's account of his psychosis.* G. Bateson, Ed. Stanford, CA: Stanford University Press.

Perry, J. W. (1974). *The far side of madness.* New York, NY: Prentice-Hall, Inc.

Perry, J. W. (1987). *The self in psychotic process: Its symbolization in schizophrenia.* Dallas, TX: Spring Publications.

Rappaport, M., Hopkins, H. K., Hall, K., Belleza, T., & Silverman, J. (1978). Are there schizophrenics for whom drugs may be unnecessary or contraindicated? *International Pharmacopsychiatry, 13,* 100–111.

Roberts, C. (1999, October). I'm hungry for reality. *Uncut.* Republished January 8, 2013. Retrieved from http://www.uncut.co.uk/features/david-bowie-i-m-hungry-for-reality-part-4-27210

Sartorius, N., Jablensky, A., & Shapiro, R. (1978). Cross-cultural differences in the short-term prognosis of schizophrenic psychoses. *Schizophrenia Bulletin, 4*, 102–113.

Soskis, D., & Bowers, M. (1969). The schizophrenic experience. *The Journal of Nervous and Mental Disease, 149*(6).

Stone, A. A. (1995, December 9). Where will psychoanalysis survive? Keynote address to the American Academy of Psychoanalysis. Retrieved from http://harvardmagazine.com/1997/01/original.html

Sullivan, H. S. (1974). *Schizophrenia as a human process.* New York, NY: W. W. Norton and Company.

Thomas, L. (1995). *The medusa and the snail.* New York, NY: Penguin Books.

Turner, V. (1987). Betwixt and between: The liminal period in *rites de passage.* In L. C. Mahdi, S. Foster, & M. Little (Eds.), *Betwixt and between: Patterns of masculine and feminine initiation.* Evanston, IL: Open Court.

Van Putten, T., & May, P. R. A. (1976). Milieu therapy of the schizophrenias. In L. J. West & D. E. Flynn (Eds.), *Treatment of schizophrenia: Progress and prospects.* New York, NY: Grune and Stratton.

Watkins, M. (2000). *Invisible guests: The development of imaginal dialogues.* Woodstock, CT: Spring Publications.

Whitaker, R. (2002). *Mad in America: Bad science, bad medicine, and the enduring mistreatment of the mentally ill.* New York, NY: Basic Books.

Whitmont, E. (1979). *The symbolic quest: Basic concepts of analytical psychology.* Princeton, NJ: Princeton University Press.

FURTHER READING

INTRODUCTION

Jung, C. G. (1969). *The structure and dynamics of the psyche. Collected works of C. G. Jung, volume 8.* Princeton, NJ: Princeton University Press.

Jung, C. G. (2009). *The red book.* S. Shamdasani (Ed.). New York, NY: W. W. Norton and Company.

FROZEN HEALERS

Benson, H. (1996). *Timeless healing: The power and biology of belief.* New York, NY: Scribner.

Cousins, N. (1981). *Anatomy of an illness.* New York, NY: Bantam Books.

Frank, J. (1991). *Persuasion and healing: A comparative study of psychotherapy.* Baltimore, MD: The Johns Hopkins University Press.

JUNG'S LAMENT

Bosnak, R. (1986). *A little course on dreams.* Boston, MA: Shambhala.

Bosnak, R. (1996). *Tracks in the wilderness of dreaming.* New York, NY: Delacorte Press.

Diamond, J., & Jones, L. S. (2004). *A path made by walking: Process work in practice.* Portland, OR: Lao Tse Press.

Hillman, J. (1983). *Healing fiction.* Woodstock, CT: Spring Publications.

Jung, A., Michel, R., Gerber, I., Ganz, D., & Ruegg, A. (2009). *The house of C. G. Jung: The history and restoration of the residence of Emma and Carl Gustav Jung-Rauschenbach.* Küsnacht, Switzerland: Stiftung C. G. Jung.

Lockhart, R. (1982). *Psyche speaks: A Jungian approach to self and world.* Wilmette, IL: Chiron.

Mindell, A. (1985a). *River's way: The process science of the dreambody.* London, England: Routledge & Kegan Paul.

Mindell, A. (1985b). *Working with the dreaming body.* Boston, MA: Routledge & Kegan Paul.

Mindell, A. (2000). *Quantum mind: The edge between physics and psychology.* Portland, OR: Lao Tse Press.

Mindell, A. (2005). *The dreaming source of creativity.* Portland, OR: Lao Tse Press.

Mindell, A., & Mindell, A. (2001). *Riding the horse backwards: Process work in theory and practice.* Portland, OR: Lao Tse Press.

Patrizia, P. (Ed.). (1999). *Authentic movement: Essays by Mary Starks Whitehouse, Janet Adler, & Joan Chodorow.* London, England, & Philadelphia, PA: Jessica Kingsley Publishers.

THERAPY AND THE ACT OF CHARACTERIZATION

Jung, C. G. (2009). *The red book.* S. Shamdasani, Ed. New York, NY: W. W. Norton and Company.

ANIMAL EYES

Alanen, Y. O., (2011). *Schizophrenia: Its origins and need-adapted treatment.* London, England: Karnac Books.

Alanen, Y. O., Gonzalez de Chavez, M., Silver, A., & Martindale, B. (Eds.). (2009). *Psychotherapeutic approaches to schizophrenic psychoses:*

Past, present and future. London, England, & New York, NY: Routledge.

Barnes, M., & Berke, J. (1978). *Mary Barnes: Two accounts of a journey through madness.* New York, NY: Ballantine Books.

Bentall, R. P. (Ed.). (1990). *Reconstructing schizophrenia.* London, England: Routledge.

Boisen, A. (1971). *The exploration of the inner world: A study of mental disorder and religious experience.* Philadelphia, PA: University of Pennsylvania Press.

Bosnak, R. (1996). *Tracks in the wilderness of dreaming.* New York, NY: Delacorte Press.

Cullberg, J. (2014). *Psychoses: An integrative perspective.* London, England, & New York, NY: Routledge.

Gale, J., Realpe, A., & Pedriali, E. (Eds.). (2013). *Therapeutic communities for psychosis: Philosophy, history and clinical practice.* London, England, & New York, NY: Routledge.

Garfield, D. (2009). *Unbearable affect: A guide to the psychotherapy of psychosis.* London, England: Karnac Books.

Garfield, D., & Steinman, I. (2015). *Self psychology and psychosis: The development of the self during intensive psychotherapy of schizophrenia and other psychoses.* London, England: Karnac Books.

The Gestalt Legacy Project. (2014). *The life and practice of Richard Price: A gestalt biography.* LuLu.com.

Gleeson, J., Killackey, E., & Krstev, H. (Eds.). (2008). *Psychotherapies of the psychoses: Theoretical, cultural and clinical integration.* London, England, & New York, NY: Routledge.

Harner, M. (1990). *The way of the shaman.* San Francisco, CA: HarperSanFrancisco.

Hopper, K., & Wanderling, J. (2000). Revisiting the developed versus developing country distinction in course and outcome in schizophrenia: Results from ISoS, the WHO collaborative followup project. *Schizophrenia Bulletin, 26*(4), 835–846.

Jackson, M. (2001). *Weathering the storms: Psychotherapy for psychosis.* London, England: Karnac Books.

Kane, J. M., Robinson, D. G., Schooler, N. R., Mueser, K. T., Penn, D. L., Rosenheck, R. A., ...Heinssen, R. K. (2016). Comprehensive versus usual community care for first-episode psychosis: 2-year outcomes from the NIMH RAISE Early Treatment Program. *The American Journal of Psychiatry, 173*(4), 362–372.

Laing, R. D. (1971). *The politics of experience.* New York, NY: Ballantine Books.

Lockhart, R. A. (2012). Mary's dog is an ear mother: Listening to the voices of psychosis. In *Words as eggs: Psyche in language and clinic.* Everett, WA: Lockhart Press.

Martindale, B., Bateman, A., Crowe, M., & Margison, F. (Eds.). (2000). *Psychosis: Psychological approaches and their effectiveness.* London, England: Gaskell.

Mendaglio, S. (Ed.). (2008). *Dabrowski's theory of positive disintegration.* Scottsdale, AZ: Great Potential Press.

Mindell, A. (1993). *The shaman's body: A new shamanism for transforming health, relationships, and the community.* San Francisco, CA: HarperSanFrancisco.

Mindell, A. (2009). *City shadows: Psychological interventions in psychiatry.* Portland, OR: Lao Tse Press.

Mosher, L., & Hendrix, V. (2004). *Soteria: Through madness to delivery.* Bloomington, IN: Xlibris.

Perry, J. W. (1961). Image, complex and transference in schizophrenia. In A. Burton, Ed., *Psychotherapy of the psychoses.* New York, NY: Basic Books.

Perry, J. W. (1967). *The heart of history: Individuality in evolution.* Albany, NY: State University of New York Press.

Perry, J. W. (1998). *Trials of the visionary mind.* Albany, NY: State University of New York Press.

Schreber, D. P. (2000). *Memoirs of my nervous illness.* New York, NY: New York Review of Books.

Silverman, J. (1967). Shamans and acute schizophrenia. *American Anthropologist, 69,* 21–31.

Steinman, I. (2009). *Treating the "untreatable": Healing in the realms of madness.* London, England: Karnac Books.

Whitaker, R. (2011). *Anatomy of an epidemic: Magic bullets, psychiatric drugs, and the astonishing rise of mental illness in America.* New York, NY: Broadway Paperbacks.

AL DE HALF'S SEPARATE REALITY

Alanen, Y. O. (2011). *Schizophrenia: Its origins and need-adapted treatment.* London, England: Karnac Books.

Crick, F. & Mitchison, G. (1983). The function of dream sleep. *Nature, 304,* 111–114.

Cullberg, J. (2014). *Psychoses: An integrative perspective.* London, England, & New York, NY: Routledge.

Gale, J., Realpe, A., & Pedriali, E. (Eds.). (2013). *Therapeutic communities for psychosis: Philosophy, history and clinical practice.* London, England, & New York, NY: Routledge.

Mindell, Amy. (2001). *Metaskills: The spiritual art of therapy.* Portland, OR: Lao Tse Press.

Mindell, Arnold. (1992). *The leader as martial artist: An introduction to deep democracy.* San Francisco, CA: HarperSanFrancisco.

THE BEARDED MAN

Jung, C. G. (1975). *Letters, Vol. 2: 1951–1961.* G. Adler & A. Jaffé, Eds. Princeton, NJ: Princeton University Press.

Mindell, A. (1982). *Dreambody: The body's role in revealing the self.* Boston, MA: Sigo Press.

INDEX

ABOUT THE AUTHOR

George Mecouch, D.O., is an osteopath and board-certified psychiatrist currently working as the medical director of a community mental health center in Washington. He also maintains a small, analytically oriented private practice with an emphasis on dream work in Vancouver, Washington, and also in Sisters, Oregon. Dr. Mecouch is currently an adjunct assistant professor of psychiatry for Pacific Northwest University of Health Sciences.

He was a student at the C G Jung Institute of Chicago in the 1980s before moving to the Portland, Oregon, area in 1990 to study process-oriented psychology with Arnold Mindell. He has authored numerous articles for online journals, blogs, and psychology journals, with a special emphasis on dreams, Jungian psychology, and psychosis. *While Psychiatry Slept* is his first book.

George Mecouch lives in Vancouver and Sisters with his wife Susan.